Silke Behling

Get to Know
Horse Breeds

The 100 Best-Known Breeds

Contents

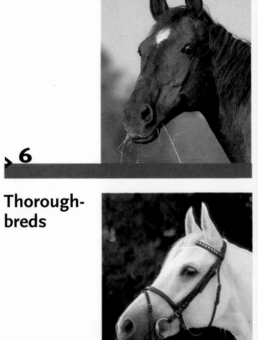

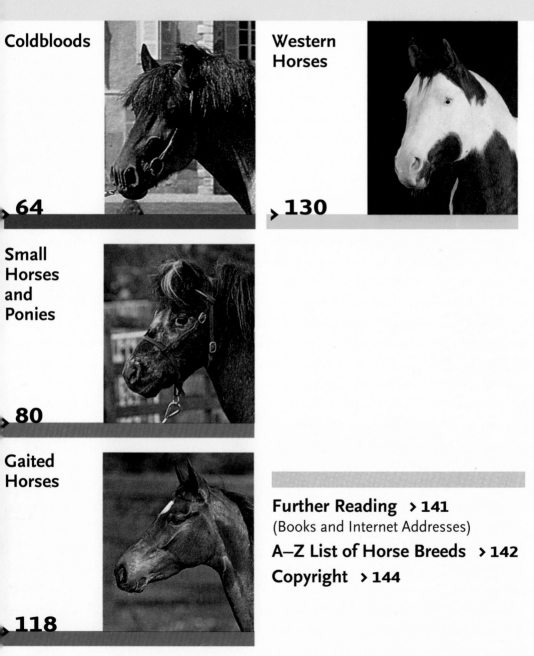

Horses

Humans have bred almost countless breeds from the original Eohippus horse, which existed during the Eocene epoch. Since ancient times, people have crossed different horse breeds to produce animals that quickly became essential for humans. Nowadays, there are a wide range of breeds that include small, compact mountain ponies; large, powerful, sure-footed animals capable of carrying enormous loads; lightning-fast racehorses; and sport horses able to perform gravity-defying jumps.

There is a horse for almost every purpose and requirement. We should remember, however, that a horse is a living thing with its own needs. In addition to being a useful animal, it is also an animal that needs our care, and we as owners should take full responsibility for the welfare of our horses.

The many different horse breeds are separated into the following seven groups according to build, weight, temperament, and genetic makeup: warmbloods, Thoroughbreds, Baroque horses, coldbloods, ponies and small horses, gaited horses, and Western horses. Of course, the Thoroughbreds, warmbloods, and coldbloods do not literally have different blood temperatures, but their temperaments do differ. A Thoroughbred behaves differently from a coldblood; it is more spirited than the coldblood,

⌃ **Warmblood horses are bred widely in Germany.**

⌄ **Horses come in all different colors and sizes.**

▼ Donkeys are also equine animals.

⌄ Thoroughbreds have a pleasant nature and are considered to be very good with people.

which does not literally have cold blood, but is generally calmer and quieter. The coldblood horses can keep their head in challenging situations and are surprisingly calm and "cool."

The temperament of a horse is crucial, as well as its abilities for different types of riding; certain horse breeds are suited to a particular type of rider. It is not only the external traits, such as color, abilities, and talents, that are important but also the internal traits that make up the character of a particular horse. Who is suitable for which horse depends largely on the individual, but one thing is for sure—certain breeds are far more suited to certain types of people.

But whether you find yourself being inspired by the more peaceful representatives of the horse world or simply fascinated by the incredibly swift racehorses, each breed has its own special qualities just waiting to be discovered.

Warmbloods

‹ Young warmbloods often grow up together in large paddocks.

› Warmbloods are the jumpers among horses.

›› Warmbloods are also very talented at dressage.

Warmblood horses were originally used in the cavalry, to pull coaches, and as riding horses. Today's sport warmbloods have been bred from the former heavy working horses and crossed with Thoroughbreds. Since the end of World War II, warmbloods have been refined to become the breeds we know today. The heavy warmblood types, such as the old Württemberg, have almost completely disappeared, so warmblood sport horses are now a rather uniform breed. A warmblood has a long back and slightly sloping shoulders and hindquarters that are incredibly strong, making this breed a talented show jumper.

Warmblood breeds are widespread. There are many breeding associations that breed them and often exchange approved mares and stallions to improve the breeds. Warmbloods have become well known because of their performances in both large and small sports tournaments around the world. You can spot them at national and international dressage and show jumping events, whose disciplines have, almost exclusively, warmblood horses taking part. They are the undisputed stars of the horse world. Some examples of warmblood horse breeds are the Hanoverian, Westphalia, Trakehner, Kinsky horse, and the Akhal-Teke.

> To Whom Are Warmbloods Suited?

Warmblood horses are ideal for those who are interested in participating in dressage or show jumping events. Because breeders place a lot of value on the ideal build and physique for horse riding, most warmbloods are very talented sport horses. A warmblood usually has an extensive stride, a trot with plenty of drive from the hindquarters, and a distinctive canter.

Of course, all this power and strength comes at a price: warmbloods are not always easy to ride, and beginners can have a difficult time keeping their balance on these spirited horses. For most beginners, a warmblood with a lively gait would be unsuitable.

Apart from that, there are warmblood breeds for almost every taste. There are just as many friendly, fearless pleasure and leisure horses as there are lively, spirited show jumping stars that require more ambitious riders. However, if you would prefer a more manageable horse to call your own, a warmblood is not necessarily right for you. At more than sixty-five inches tall, most warmbloods are very large!

Akhal-Teke

Height: 59–63 inches

Color: all colors, usually chestnut or various shades of brown with copper shimmer

Origin: Central Asia

The Akhal-Teke is thought to be one of the oldest horse breeds in the world.

Just to give a sense of how tall each horse breed is at the withers (shoulders), the person in the diagram is about 6 feet tall.

The Akhal-Teke is thought to have been around since 500 B.C. This breed is exceptionally noble and extremely fast. The Akhal-Teke is praised for its enormous perseverance, insensitivity to heat, and frugal eating habits. This horse has a natural predisposition to a fluid, even, and clean gait.

In the high plains of Central Asia, this ancient breed of horse was bred in pre-Christian times. It is said Akhal-Tekes were used by the guards of King Darius of Persia in 500 B.C. These elegant horses have a long, lightly muscled back that connects to a flat croup, or rump. Their ribs are relatively flat, but their muscles are amazingly well adapted. The erect, upright position of the head and the long neck are typical of Akhal-Tekes. Their skin is particularly thin, and the coat is very fine. The brown, fallow, or chestnut coat often has a metallic gold or copper shimmer, similar to that of Kinsky horses.

Altér Real

Height: 59–63 inches
Color: brown
Origin: Alentejo, Portugal

Altér Reals are almost exclusively brown.

In 1748, in Portugal, the first Altér Real stud originated from Andalusian mares from Jerez, Spain. Breeding of Altér Reals almost came to a standstill in the nineteenth century when French emperor Napoléon Bonaparte stole most of the horses. The breed was built up once again using Andalusian mares. However, the future of Altér Reals remained uncertain. In the early twentieth century, the studbook, or official record of the pedigree of purebred horses, was dissolved and did not start up again until 1942.

The Altér Real is actually a branch of the Lusitano breed. Head profiles vary from straight to convex, with very upright necks, short backs, and lightly sloping hindquarters. This affords them a good balance and an excellent center of gravity, which is why Altér Reals are suited to dressage and classical dressage.

Bavarian Warmblood

Height: 64–67 inches

Color: brown, chestnut, and more rarely white and black

Origin: Bavaria

The Bavarian warmblood originates from the Rottaler breed.

Rottalers have been bred in Bavaria since about A.D. 1000. The Rottaler is a medium-sized, heavy, all-purpose horse and is a highly endangered breed

Bavarian warmbloods are bred today for both leisure activities and tournaments.

nowadays. The heavy warmbloods were previously selected for breeding according to the following criteria: performance, willingness to cooperate, and suitability for riding. From the 1950s onward, the Rottaler no longer corresponded to the desired horse type—the lighter build of a sport horse—so the breed was refined using Hanoverian, Westphalian, Trakehner, and other warmblood stallions. The resulting Bavarian warmblood barely differs from the other German warmblood breeds. The Bavarian warmblood stud farm is in Schwaiganger, Bavaria, and has a number of privately owned stallions. The studbook in Schwaiganger has a long tradition: young horses have been reared in Schwaiganger since 1808. This stud farm for Bavarian warmbloods still exists today. Haflingers and coldbloods are also bred there.

Belgian Warmblood

Height: from 63 inches
Color: all colors
Origin: Belgium

The Belgian warmblood is
still a relatively new breed.

After World War II, systematic importing of sport horses began in Belgium in an attempt to build up a uniquely Belgian breed. In 1955, the Belgian Breeding Association, known as the National Fokvereniging van het Warmbloedpaard (NFWP), was founded. Four thousand mares and stallions from private breeders now belong to this organization. Breeders specifically selected horses with show jumping talent: Gelderlanders from Holland, Norman horses from France, and Hanoverians from Germany formed the basis of the breed. Targeted breeding resulted in a large sport horse with a slightly less noble bearing than other warmblood breeds.

The Belgian warmblood predominantly celebrates successes in show jumping, and they are also in high demand internationally by beginner riders. From the early 1970s, Belgian breeders tested colts' performances for show jumping. Because the main focus of the breed was jumping abilities, other disciplines were neglected. Some say that Belgian warmbloods can be problematic to ride, so they are seldom found in classical dressage events. They are generally too heavy for certain events. The stud farm for Belgian warmbloods is in Zangersheide, Belgium, but there are also many farmers who breed Belgian warmbloods.

Brandenburger and Mecklenburger

Height: 64–67 inches

Color: brown, chestnut, black

Origin: Brandenburg and Mecklenburg, Germany

Brandenburgers and Mecklenburgers are very similar breeds.

In the former German Democratic Republic (East Germany), breeders aimed to breed warmbloods able to compete with other internationally successful German warmblood breeds. Currently, these two breeds are not as successful as the sport horses from West German breeds. Their outward appearance is very similar to other Western European warmblood breeds, except for slightly different markings. With respect to their performance, the Brandenburger's and Mecklenburger's jumping abilities are not as outstanding as that of the Holsteiner breed, for example.

Breeding of Mecklenburgers and Brandenburgers began on a stud farm in Neustadt, Brandenburg, in 1787. English and Arabian Thoroughbreds, Trakehners and also an Akhal-Teke were used to establish the breed. The stud farm was a success leading up to World War II; cavalry horses were particularly in demand. The Brandenburger is lighter than the Mecklenburger. The Brandenburger is closely related to the Trakehner and has a lively temperament and a lot of energy. The Mecklenburger is reminiscent of the old type of heavy Hanoverian breed. It is fairly straightforward to handle and is therefore very popular with less athletic riders.

Brandenburgers have become more and more of a talking point in international equestrian tournaments. Some are very successful show jumpers.

British Warmblood

Height: 64–67 inches
Color: all colors
Origin: England

The British warmblood breed began in the 1970s.

British warmbloods are a very new breed. It has existed since the 1970s and was created by crossing various European warmblood breeds, including German warmbloods. Dutch, Swedish, and Danish warmbloods were also imported to create a modern sport horse breed that would perform well in tournaments. Studbooks and performance tests were used to achieve and maintain high quality and performance standards.

Outwardly, the British warmblood does not differ significantly from other warmbloods. It has a medium-sized head, a curved neck, a good saddle position, and a slightly flat croup. Its gait and jumping ability are consistent with other modern sport horse breeds.

13

Budyonny

Height: about 63 inches

Color: mainly chestnut and brown, no white

Origin: Russia

A Budyonny's coat has a beautiful gold sheen.

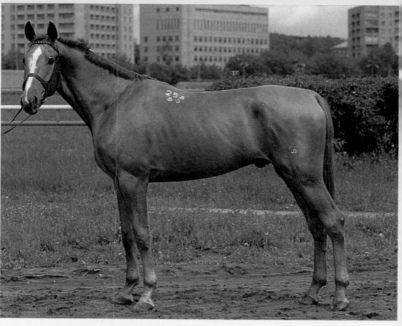

A Cossack general named Sergej Budjonny bred Budyonnys from Russian Dons and English Thoroughbreds. Budyonnys were bred as cavalry horses. In addition to exhibiting good riding properties, Budyonnys also make ideal harness horses. They have also participated in sports tournaments since World War II.

Because of their high proportion of Thoroughbred blood, Budyonnys tend to be temperamental. It also makes them suitable for long-distance rides as well as the steeplechase. They have participated in the Olympic Games in dressage and jumping events. Budyonnys originated from an inhospitable desert area by the Don River in Russia, where they lived in herds and were allowed to roam free. The living conditions in the steppe are tough; the horses are alternately exposed to heat, cold, drought, and insect infestations, but Budyonnys are remarkably well adapted to these difficult conditions.

Budyonnys have a talent for jumping.

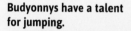

Cleveland Bay

Height: 64–68 inches
Color: brown
Origin: England

Cleveland bays are ideally brown (English bay). Markings are undesirable.

Cleveland bays are considered an endangered breed. However, the Queen of England is involved in the preservation of the breed; Cleveland bays are used to pull carriages in royal processions. Cleveland bays were bred as packhorses in the seventh century by the Abbots of Whitby, a Benedictine order of monks. The horses originated from a crossing between Arabians, Andalusians, and Berber horses. This medium-sized, brown horse has a large head with a slightly convex profile and is powerful with relatively short legs. This horse breed is extremely hardworking and fast and also undemanding, healthy, and hardy. Some Cleveland bays are still used as workhorses well after the age of twenty. In the nineteenth century, Cleveland bays were used for the breeding of almost all other European warmblood breeds. But they no longer comply with the modern sport horse ideal, and so the breed is threatened with extinction.

A Cleveland bay in the paddock is, sadly, a rare sight nowadays.

15

Cob

Height: 55–61 inches

Color: all colors

Origin: United Kingdom

Cob is an old English word meaning "small, powerful horse."

These two powerful cobs are capable of carrying very heavy loads.

Cobs are strong, somewhat squat horses, larger than ponies but smaller than most other horse breeds. In Germany, these horses are known as *Doppelponys*, literally "double ponies."

The English cob is a crossbreed that was bred in a haphazard way. They originated from a cross between Thoroughbred stallions and Highland, Dales, or Connemara pony mares or with strong ponies from the local area. There are different types of cob: the show cob, the driving cob, and the riding cob.

A particularly special type from this breed is the Northumberland cob, a cross between Hackneys and Welsh cobs. This type makes an excellent driving horse or carriage horse.

Cobs have attractive faces, well-muscled backs, and strong, wide croups. They are powerful and can easily carry a heavy rider. In addition, most cobs jump quite well, meaning they are very fast during hunts.

Danish Warmblood

Height: 64–67 inches
Color: all colors
Origin: Denmark

Danish warmbloods are very similar to other European warmbloods.

Danish warmbloods are a relatively new breed that began in 1962. Previously, horse breeding in Denmark was very focused around the stud farms of Frederiksborg and Kolding. When the studbook was dissolved at the end of the nineteenth century, Danish horses were bred by private breeders, often resulting in temperamental draft and workhorses, so in 1962 it was decided to systematically breed a type of modern riding and sport horse. The Danes used stallions from Germany, Sweden, England, and Poland as the basis for this modern sport horse. The Danish warmblood soon became more popular than the Hanoverian and Trakehner. Thanks to the studs imported to Denmark, this breed became internationally successful in dressage and other events. One such example is the gelding owned by Anne Grethe Jensen named Marzog, which won the world cup in dressage in 1985. Danish warmbloods are known to be particularly friendly and are ideal for recreational riders because they are relatively straightforward and unproblematic.

To date, Danish warmbloods are predominantly bred by private breeders in Denmark.

This sport horse can accelerate extremely well.

Russian Don

Height: 61–63 inches

Color: usually brown and chestnut

Origin: Russia

Like other Eastern horse breeds, the Russian Don has a gold shimmer to its coat.

The first Russian Don stud farm was founded in 1770. Among others, the Russian Don was bred with the Tarpan horse, a now extinct breed of wild horse.

Russian Dons are also popular recreational horses.

The earlier Russian Don was therefore not very large or hardy.

Countless breeds have played a role in the emergence of today's Russian Don: Turkmens, Arabians, and Kabardins, as well as English Thoroughbreds and Orlov Rostopschiners. Russian Dons have been bred systematically since the beginning of the nineteenth century, especially as cavalry horses for the military. Breeders began to use a selection criteria for a set standard of appearance, but they also sought other characteristics such as endurance, health, frugality, and jumping ability. Consequently, Russian Dons are excellent sport horses, just as successful at jumping as they are at dressage. Their best discipline is most certainly endurance racing. During a race in 1950, a group of Russian Don stallions famously covered a distance of one hundred ninety miles in twenty hours.

Frederiksborger

Height: 63 inches
Color: mainly chestnut
Origin: Denmark

Frederiksborgers usually have large white markings and a lighter-colored mane.

The Frederiksborger's glory days were between the sixteenth and eighteenth centuries, where he served as a showpiece in Denmark and throughout Europe. The foundation of Danish horse breeding was begun by King Friedrich II in 1560 with the royal Frederiksborger stud farm in Copenhagen. Indigenous Spanish horses and Neapolitan stallions were imported to Denmark to refine the breed. Thus the Frederiksborger had the coveted leg action and perfectly upright position that is particularly desirable in Baroque dressage. The influence of the Neapolitan and Iberians can also be seen in the often slightly convex head shape of the Frederiksborger. In the late nineteenth century, the baroque type of Frederiksborger unfortunately fell victim to inbreeding experiments as a workhorse and later as a sport horse, so it is counted today as an endangered species.

A rare sight today, the Frederiksborger is now threatened with extinction.

Furioso

Height: 63 inches

Color: brown only

Origin: Hungary

Furioso horses originated from a Thoroughbred born in 1835 named Furioso.

The Furioso-North Star is a medium-sized warmblood horse. The foundation stock studs of the breed were the Thoroughbred stallions Furioso, born in 1835, and North Star, born in 1844. These two studs were used to create a new breed in the Hungarian town of Mezöhegyes. The breed not only made an ideal riding horse but was also suitable for light agricultural work.

The two stallions each founded their own bloodline; however, in 1885, these bloodlines became one, hence the combined name Furioso-North Star.

The North Star line has lost its meaning over time; the Furioso name is now mostly used to refer to the breed. After World War II, attempts were made to refine the Furioso breed by crossing it with other Thoroughbred and warmblood breeds to try to breed a sport horse suitable for tournaments.

As a consequence, the purebred Furiosos are now almost extinct. The resulting modern horse breed was only moderately successful in tournaments. However, this modern breed has contributed to the refining of Hungarian horse breeds, resulting in the closure of the studbook and the relocation of the stud farm from Mezöhegyes to Apajpuszta.

Individual private breeders continue to breed Furiosos in and outside of Hungary, and Furiosos are also crossed with Leutstetten horses in Bavaria, which is an indirect continuation of the bloodline. Leutstetten horses were originally called Sárvár but have been renamed after their new native Bavaria. Some of the descendants of the Furioso have inherited their unusual markings—very bright white spots on their abdomens.

Hackney

Height: 59–63 inches
Color: brown, black, chestnut
Origin: England

Hackneys are the ballerinas among the carriage horses.

The name Hackney is thought to have come from the medieval French word *haquenée*, which was the name of a lightweight riding horse for women. Today's breed of Hackney, however, has little to do with the medieval horse other than the fact it is used for riding. The breed began in the early eighteenth century, originating from two draft horse breeds, the Yorkshire trotter and Norfolk roadster, and the foundation stud stallion Shales, a great-grandson of the famous Darley, an Arabian horse. The Hackney is a medium-sized horse with a charming face, small head, a high-set neck, and steep shoulders. Their most striking characteristic is their spectacular trot. This is partly innate and partly trained, emphasized with specialized shoeing. In 1878, a breeding organization was created specially for Hackneys and the studbook began in 1883. Hackney ponies, formerly known as Wilson ponies, are included in this studbook. They are between fifty-one and fifty-eight inches tall. The Shot Fell pony is classified as a Hackney pony.

Hackney horses are known for their spectacular front leg trotting action.

21

Gelderlander and Groninger

Height: 65 inches

Color: brown or chestnut

Origin: Netherlands

The Gelderlander and Groninger are Dutch workhorse breeds.

Gelderlanders and Groningers were originally the same breed of horse and were bred from native horses, Oldenburgers, Holsteiners, Normans, and Norfolk trotters. Both were relatively heavy agricultural and working horses used on farms.

The Gelderlander, from the southern part of the Netherlands, is somewhat lighter than the Groninger, which had to cope with plowing heavy soil in the north. As the name suggests, the Gelderlander breed originates from the province of Gelderland in the Netherlands. From the 1960s, as the demand for agricultural workhorses decreased, the Gelderlanders were bred to become a more lightweight type of horse. Gelderlanders tend to have a convex head profile and a deep chest. They are usually brown or chestnut in color and are not as large as modern sport horses; they rarely exceed sixty-five inches in height. The Groningers, however, are similar to the heavy Alt-Oldenburgers and the imposing Friesians and are somewhat heavier than the Gelderlanders.

The old type of Groninger owes its existence to a breeding association that campaigned for its preservation, but despite these efforts, their number is greatly diminished nowadays. Perhaps its friendly temperament will help its popularity to rise again; recreational riders appreciate the amiable Groninger. Their gentle nature and their strength, expressed by their high leg action, also mean they are ideal driving horses. The Gelderlander's and Groninger's trot is particularly pronounced; their other gaits sometimes seem more subtle. Both breeds are the foundation for the Dutch warmblood and will therefore continue to be bred for this purpose. Crossing these two breeds with Thoroughbreds or half-breeds usually produces horses with excellent jumping abilities.

23

Hanoverian

Height: 64–69 inches

Color: all colors

Origin: Hanover, Germany

One of the most well-known Hanoverian stallions is the chestnut horse named Weltmeyer.

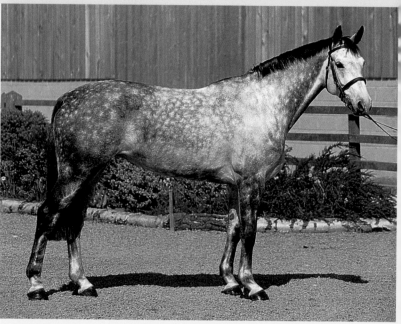

Hanoverians are world-famous dressage and show jumping horses. Like all warmbloods, they were originally bred for fieldwork and earned their daily oats by plowing the fields.

The heavy, old Hanoverian type tended to have a convex head profile and was a true workhorse used for agricultural purposes. In recent times, the Hanoverian breed was crossed with English Thoroughbreds and Trakehners, so they have become more athletic over time due to their lighter build. They are an all-purpose breed with a good temperament and agreeable character. The desired height of these large-framed warmblood horses is between sixty-four and sixty-nine inches. They are mostly chestnut brown, but there are also white and black versions. The Hanoverian breed has the largest breed population of warmblood horses worldwide. Dressage horses such as Gigolo, who won four Olympic gold medals with rider Isabell Werth, made the Hanoverian sport horses world famous.

Recreational riders around the world also appreciate the Hanoverian as an excellent show jumper.

Today there is hardly a warmblood breed that has not been influenced by the Hanoverian. Not only have they refined every other German warmblood breed, but they are also successfully used for sport horse breeding throughout Europe.

Many Hanoverian horses are fortunate enough to grow up in the vast pastures of Lower Saxony in Germany.

The Trakehner's temperament is still evident in today's Hanoverian horses.

Hessian Warmblood

Height: 63–67 inches

Color: brown, black, white, chestnut

Origin: Hessen, Germany

The ancestors of the Hessian warmbloods were called the Dillenburger Ramsnasen.

The most famous Hessian warmblood is the mare Halla; Hans Günter Winkler, her rider, received the gold medal at the Olympics in 1956. Halla's father was a Trakehner and her mother was a French horse breed. She was therefore a very typical warmblood—a cross between different sport horse lines. Hessian warmbloods are about sixty-three to sixty-seven inches tall and usually brown, white, black, or chestnut. The breed has an attractive face, long neck, and good saddle position. The strong back and the slightly sloping croup are characteristics of the Hessian as well as all other sport horses. The Hessian warmblood is a German riding horse and is fairly similar to other German warmblood breeds. The Hessian is a relatively small breed with some twenty-five hundred registered mares. In the eighteenth century, the Dillenburg stud was decorated as the Hessian-Nassau royal stud. The first serious workhorses of Oldenburg and East Frisia were bred from him to create the so-called "Dillenburger Ramsnasen (Roman nose)," the ancestor of the Hessian breed.

In 1962, modern sport horse breeding was moved to Hessen. Stallions from other breeding areas, especially Hanoverians and Trakehners, were used to refine the Hessian breed.

In 2005, the Hessian breeding association formed an alliance with the Hanoverian breed association. By 2009, the resulting foals had Hessian markings.

Holsteiner

Height: 64–69 inches

Color: mainly brown and black; chestnut and white are fairly rare

Origin: Holstein, Germany

Holsteiners are sought worldwide for their show jumping abilities.

The jumping ability of the Holsteiner warmbloods is legendary, so these great sport horses are in high demand all over the world. At the Olympic Games in Athens in 2004, five Holsteiners won medals for their riders. Holsteiners are known to be faithful and reliable, and although they are hardworking and eager, they are rarely hyperactive.

Holsteiners have been around since the Middle Ages, and like so many other horse breeds, were crossed with Spanish horses. Nowadays, English Thoroughbreds and half bloods are used for the continuation of the breed. Cottage Son and Ladykiller are famous Thoroughbreds of the Holsteiner breed. Ladykiller himself was only moderately successful at racing, but with thirty-five approved sons, he was one of the most famous sires of the breed.

27

Hunter and Irish Hunter

Height: 59–69 inches

Color: all colors

Origins: England and Ireland

Hunters were not deliberately bred; they originated from all-purpose workhorses.

Hunters do not necessarily conform to a special breed standard but are bred according to their all-around suitability. Therefore, they are not all uniform, and there are lighter and heavier types of build. In the United Kingdom, hunters are officially divided into light, middle, and heavy classes.

Generally, hunters are heavier than many other warmbloods and during trials, they must prove that they can bear a large amount of weight.

Because of the "random" breeding of hunters, the horse's performance counts for more than his origin. Irish hunters are said to have a better jumping ability than the English hunters, while the English hunters have a greater proportion of Thoroughbred blood.

Kinsky

Height: 63–65 inches
Color: dun and pale fawn
Origin: Czech Republic

Kinskys are also called Bohemian hunters, which refers to their talent as hunting horses.

Kinsky horses have a sleek build with a high proportion of pure blood. You can tell a Kinsky horse by its unusual color and shimmering coat. Kinsky horses are mainly a light dun or a pale fawn. In the eighteenth century, the Czech king commissioned the Kinsky family of counts to breed horses for the military and agriculture. Horses from this breed were also used for hunting because they usually possessed good jumping abilities.

Back then, just as today, people were fascinated by horses with lustrous coats. The characteristic shimmering coat of the Kinsky arises from a genetic defect. In Kinsky horses, the hair shaft of each individual hair is very thin. This creates a layer between the thin shaft and the so-called outer hair cortex from which the light is reflected. This results in a very shiny metallic sheen on the coat. It is the actual structure of the hair that causes the shimmer, not a genetic color. This particular coat texture is sometimes seen in other breeds, such as Akhal-Tekkers, Arabian horses, English Thoroughbreds, Tersk horses, and Budyonnys.

Kinskys are very rare. It is suspected that there are only about three hundred fifty to four hundred of them left in the world. Most of these live in their Czech homeland on the stud farm Chlumec nad Cidlinou. Kinskys tend to be very people oriented and are very willing and calm, which is why they are so popular with recreational riders. Their long-stride canter is particularly good for longer distances.

Maremmano

Height: 58–62 inches

Color: usually black or dark brown

Origin: Italy

Maremmanos are the horses of Italian shepherds.

The home of the Maremmanos is on the coast of the Tyrrhenian Sea.

The full name of the Maremmano breed is Maremmano Tolfetano. This breed has always been ridden by shepherds of the Maremma Lanziale, an alluvial plain on the west coast of Italy, next to the Tyrrhenian Sea. The shepherds in that region are called the "Butteri."

This ancient breed has been around since approximately 900–300 B.C. They are semiwild, thus Maremmanos have preserved their hardiness and their resistance to heat and cold. Because of this incredible hardiness, they are also occasionally called "East Prussian Italians," which is a reference to the much acclaimed features of the Trakehner. In recent times, Maremmanos have been increasingly crossed with Thoroughbreds in order to produce sport horses that are popular with the Italian Carabinieri, the national military police of Italy. In equestrian tournaments, Maremmanos can more than match the talents of other warmblood horses. The specially bred Maremmanos are slightly larger than their original relatives and often reach sixty-five inches in height.

Dutch Warmblood

Height: 65–69 inches
Color: all colors
Origin: Netherlands

Dutch warmbloods are also known as KWPN riding horses.

Dutch riding horses are also referred to as KWPN, which stands for *Koninklijke Warmbloed Paardenstamboek in Nederland* and is the official name of the Dutch studbook. The mares originated from Gelderlander and Groninger horses while the stallions originated from other warmblood breeds including those from north Germany. French Normans and English Thoroughbreds were also used to refine the breed. There are differences between the sport horse, the harness horse, and the Gelderlander type. The sport horse is bred to excel in dressage and jumping. The harness horse has a proud, upright head position and high knee action. The Gelderlander has retained the typical qualities of a draft horse. Since the 1960s, very stringent selection criteria for broodmares and stallions has meant that the Dutch warmblood has evolved into an internationally successful sport horse. Famous representatives of the breed include the chestnut horse named Ideal, the Grand Prix dressage horse belonging to German equestrian Sven Rothenberger, and the famous stallion Marius, owned by English rider Caroline Bradley.

In addition to their excellent athletic abilities, Dutch warmbloods are also known for their pleasant, sweet-natured temperament.

Most Dutch warmbloods are brown.

31

Oldenburger

Height: 63–68 inches

Color: all colors

Origin: Oldenburg, Germany

Chestnut and white Oldenburgers are rare.

Top: White and silver dapple are far rarer than brown and black (right). One famous example was the white stud named Kranich, the favorite horse of Count Anton Günther von Oldenburg (1583–1667), and it was during his reign that Oldenburg breeding reached a high point. All three horses pictured are typical examples of modern Oldenburgers. Dappled Oldenburgers sometimes have a slightly convex head shape.

Oldenburgers are the heaviest German warmblood breed. Originally, they were bred as workhorses. This heavier breed, today called the Alt-Oldenburger, was outstandingly strong and suitable for agricultural work and pulling carriages.

By the late nineteenth century, these heavy workhorses no longer conformed to the now desirable sport horse type. Thoroughbreds, Hanoverians, and Holsteiners helped to refine this breed to become a noble sport horse with excellent jumping ability. French stallions also had an influence on the Oldenburger breed. The chestnut stallion Furioso II, born in Normandy in 1965, was the father of thirteen hundred successful competition horses. These big, strong, colorful chestnut horses still participate in show jumping events.

The heavy Alt-Oldenburger, which is closely related to the East Friesian horse, is unfortunately now endangered. Because agricultural work is now performed by machinery, there is no further demand for him and thus no future. But there is a high demand for modern sport horses. Examples of successful Oldenburgers are the mare named Weiheiwei, who won the show jumping at the 1994 World Cup with Franke Sloothaak, and Bonfire, who celebrated success with Anky van Grunsven in the 1990s dressage arenas. Today, Oldenburgers are just as successful as they are numerous; there are about eighty-five hundred broodmares registered with the breed association.

Orlov Trotter

Height: about 64 inches

Color: usually white, also brown and black

Origin: Bulgaria

This breed got its name from Count Alexei Orlov, a Russian soldier and statesman.

Above: In their youth, gray Orlovs have a particularly dappled coat.

Legend has it that in the eighteenth century, Count Orlov began a new breed of carriage horse because he had become too heavy for riding. He crossed the son of an Oriental stallion with a Danish mare and the resulting son with a Dutch mare. The resulting stallion named Bars is the father of all the Orlov trotters. The Orlov trotter is a very good coach and carriage horse with exceptional trotting action. Up to the mid-nineteenth century, the Orlov trotter was considered to be the fastest trotter in the world, until it was superseded by the American trotter. The Orlov trotter has become increasingly rare in recent years. The Russian Imperial Administration went to great efforts to save the elegant yet powerful trotter breed from extinction, and thankfully, its spectacular trot can still be admired today. Orlov trotters are also bred in Bavaria. The unusual trotting action is part of the selection criteria for breeding.

Swedish Warmblood

Height: 62–65 inches

Color: all colors; chestnut is common

Origin: Sweden

The Swedish warmblood breed has been around for three hundred years.

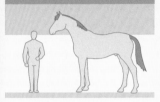

Swedish warmbloods are very similar to other European warmbloods; they are successful horse breeds in Olympic dressage events, are used for the military, and are sociable leisure horses. However, the Swedish warmblood has a particularly notable talent for jumping.

About 1700, on the royal stud farm of Flyinge, Spanish, Oriental, and Friesian breeds were crossed with the objective of creating a horse breed for the royal family and the cavalry. Over time, Arabian, Hanoverian, Trakehner, and Thoroughbred stallions were also added to the mix to improve the performance of the breed. To date, Swedish warmbloods in Flyinge are bred under state control, according to their performance. The stallions have to provide proof of their quality in strict performance tests in order to be admitted to the breeding program.

Swedish warmbloods are commonly a chestnut color with some markings, but all other colors can occur. They have relatively small heads. A height of over sixty-five inches is undesirable.

This colt displays the typical Swedish warmblood coloring: chestnut with white markings.

35

Selle Français

Height: varies

Color: mostly chestnut and brown; white is rare

Origin: France

The Selle Français is also known as the Anglo-Norman horse.

The Cheval de Selle Français, which means "French riding or saddle horse," is the official French name for these half bloods, named in 1958. Because they descended from the heavy draft horses of Normandy and belonged to the Normans, the Selle Français are also known as the Anglo-Normans.

The Norman horses are an ancient breed, originating in the seventeenth century. They also have Arabian and Berber blood, as well as genes from heavy German warmbloods. During the eighteenth and nineteenth centuries, the breed was crossed with Norfolk trotters and Thoroughbreds, which resulted in the Anglo-Norman breed.

After this, they were separated into four different types: the cob, the Karrosier, the Selle, and the trotter. The trotter is the type that still exists today. From the remaining lineage, an everyday driving and riding horse was developed with a high proportion of whole blood. Today, about one-third of all Selle Français have a Thoroughbred stallion a a father and 20 percent have an Anglo-Arabian as a sire. About 45 percent of Selle Français horses can be called purebloods. Only 2 percent of all Selle Français horses are French trotters.

The Selle Français is mainly bred as a sport horse and is known to have excellent jumping abilities. However, the Selle Français are also known for their versatility. In the Cadre Noir, an equestrian troop based in Saumur, France, some horses have shown a talent for classical dressage, and they are also successful refiners of other breeds. For example, the stallion Cor de la Bryère ha strongly influenced the Holsteiner sport horse breed.

Trotter (European)

Height: 57–65 inches

Color: all colors

Origin: Europe, primarily France

In France, trotters are also used for riding.

Trotters are bred for harness racing. They do not have a uniform type because the selection criteria for breeding is based on their race performance rather than their external appearance. Breeders of European trotters have long campaigned against the usage of the American trotter in their breed. Nevertheless, the American trotters are considered particularly fast and tough.

Bred to pull sulkies, or two-wheeled carts, some trotters have a deer-like neck and a back that is too soft for riding. Despite this, many trotters are used for recreational purposes by gaited-horse riders. Because many trotters have a predisposition to be gaited, or able to perform an ambling gait (a four-beat gait faster than a walk but slower than a canter), they can also learn to tölt, which is a smooth four-beat gait with the two legs on the same side of the horse moving together. They can also learn to run at race pace.

Trakehner

Height: 63–66 inches

Color: all colors; white is rare

Origin: East Prussia

There is a statue of the famous Trakehner stallion named Temple Guardian in Verden, Lower Saxony, Germany.

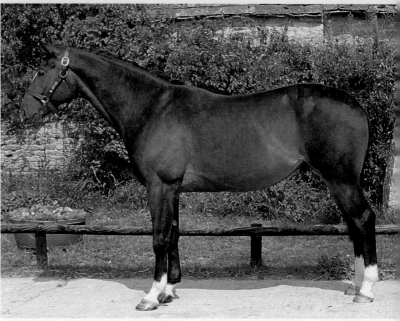

Trakehners were bred in East Prussia by the Teutonic Knights by crossing the Schweiken, the indigenous East Prussian breed, with various larger imported stallions to provide mounts for warfare, for general transportation, and for agricultural work. Trakehners are very elegant, sometimes sensitive horses, that require sensitive riders. The breed's sensitive temperament has given the Trakehners the reputation of being difficult, but in competent hands, they are very reliable. Their commitment is legendary, and Trakehners have often achieved Olympic success, especially as dressage and event horses.

During World War II, a number of horses were taken from East Prussia to Germany. Eight hundred mares and forty stallions were evacuated to the West on an adventurous journey. Trakehner coloring is noteworthy: pinto coloring (white and colored patches, often black) has long been undesirable in other breeds; however, the Trakehner is the only breed where pinto is actually permitted.

Westphalian

Height: 65–68 inches
Color: all colors
Origin: Westphalia, Germany

Westphalia is the second largest German warmblood breeding area after Hanover.

The Westphalian conforms to the modern sport horse type. It is very similar to the Hanoverian but somewhat bigger and stronger. By 1826, the studbook was founded in Warendorf, Westphalia, in the town of Münster. However, the breed struggled at first because farms in the vicinity wanted workhorses rather than sport horses.

Both warmbloods and coldbloods were bred, but by the end of World War II, heavy draft horses were in the majority. Warmbloods were mainly used as carriage horses and were initially relatively indiscriminately crossed with Oldenburgers, Hanoverians, Anglo-Normans, and trotters. From about 1920, more systematic warmblood breeding began. The Westphalian breed was based on the proven Hanoverian stallions. Because the market in the post-war period demanded more rideable show horses, in Warendorf, the Westphalian emerged as the modern sport horse type. Today, Westphalian breeders have bred a considerable number of successful horses; their ability to jump is higher than average and this breed is among the best sport horses in the world.

39

Württemberger

Height: 63–66 inches

Color: brown, black, and chestnut

Origin: Württemberg, Germany

Warmbloods and Arabian horses are bred on stud farms in the Baden-Württemberg area.

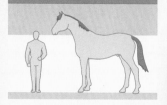

The Baden-Württemberg horse was initially bred as a hardy horse, suitable for everyday use, and well able to negotiate the mountainous areas of the Württemberg region.

To this end, the indigenous working horse was crossed with Arabian stallions from the stud farm in Marbach. The stud from the Alb area in Swabia was founded in the fifteenth century. Later it was crossed with East Prussian Trakehners, French Normans, Hungarian Verniers, and Alt-Oldenburg horses. For a short time, Württemburgers were also bred with Suffolks and Clydesdales. This colorful mixture was not a particularly successful one, but when the breeding was limited for Trakehner stallions after World War II, the breed became more promising.

At that time, the Württemberger breed was refined for the changing demands of the market and began to be bred as a modern sport horse. Under strong influence of Holsteiner stallions, the Baden-Württembergers are today warmblood horses with good dressage and jumping abilities.

Due to this crossbreeding, unfortunately the Old-Württemberger breed is nearly extinct. The old type was bred to be an all-purpose horse, strong enough for heavy work but handsome enough for riding and coachwork.

The modern Württembergers can also be seen in dressage events.

The powerful cob-type warmblood was useful at the time. However, these horses are now very rare because after World War II, breeding favored a lighter, more athletic sport type. Currently, there are only about thirty registered broodmares. The Old-Württembergers are usually slightly smaller than their sportier relatives and often brown or dark brown in color. Their trotting is often unusually good, but long-stride canters are not their specialty. The Old-Württemberger breed was crossed with Anglo-Norman stallions and mares, with some Arabian blood. These horses have won many fans with recreational riders, who consider a horse with a pleasant temperament that is easy to care for as more important than an exceptional jumping ability. The modern Württembergers compete in large sports tournaments; their all-round movements and jumping abilities are excellent.

41

Wielkopolski

Height: 64 inches

Color: all colors

Origin: Poland

Wielkopolskis originate from the Trakehner breed.

After World War II in Poland, Mazury horses were bred with the few remaining Trakehners.

The Wielkopolski was bred from these now-extinct Mazury horses and also the Posen. The Posen, also called the West Prussian, has a high percentage of Trakehner blood. Both breeds have always strongly resembled one another, so they were combined into a single breed around 1960. The Wielkopolskis are bred at thirteen large stud farms in Poland where they undergo regular performance tests. The Wielkopolski has an attractive face with a wide forehead; an upright, powerful neck; strong back; and well-defined tendons in the legs. Most Wielkopolskis are chestnut and brown; white and black are rare. There are also occasional pinto examples that carry the legacy of the Trakehner coloring.

Although the Wielkopolskis are bred systematically, they are not yet as successful as, for example, Holsteiners or Selle Français. The Wielkopolskis are very good carriage horses, and they have the strength to perform light agricultural duties; this is where they demonstrate their hard work and reliability.

Zweibrücker

Height: 63–66 inches
Color: all colors
Origin: Rheinland-Pfalz-Saar, Germany

In the sixteenth century, in Rheinland-Pfalz-Saar, breeders began to breed horses more systematically and with great success. Founded in 1755 by Duke Christian IV, the Zweibrücker studding was badly affected by the outbreak of war. However, the duke had a promising breeding plan: English Thoroughbred mares and Anglo-French Normans were crossed with Zweibrückers. After a few years, the Zweibrücker horses gained a reputation that reached far beyond the country's borders. In 1783, Frederick the Great bought over one hundred fifty Zweibrückers to refine his Trakehners. During the Napoleonic Wars, the stud was moved again. Napoleon is said to have been thrilled with the Zweibrücker horses. He reopened the studbook and contributed a stallion. The stud farm came under threat in 1945 due to World War II and was eventually destroyed by bombing. The reconstruction of the breed began using Hanoverians, Westphalians, Oldenburgers, and Holsteiners. The Zweibrückers strongly resemble these horse breeds and have the same excellent jumping abilities for dressage and show jumping.

The original Zweibrückers had Arabian blood. When they were crossbred to produce a sport horse, the proportion of Trakehner blood was very large, and ultimately breeders only used Trakehners from the stud farm Birkhausen in Pfalz to refine the breed. The amount of Zweibrückers decreased in the 1970s due to the impact of the Trakehner horse breed. However, the private stud farm Drachenhof near Koblenz has bred many successful Zweibrückers for show jumping.

Thoroughbreds

⌃ Step on the gas! Thoroughbred horses love to be put to the test.

Thoroughbreds began from the widespread Arabian horse breed. Arabian horses have been around for at least sixteen hundred years on the Arabian Peninsula and are considered to be the world's oldest breed of horse. Characteristics of the Arabian horse include a small head with a broad forehead and a distinctive concave profile. Many Arabians also have a slight bulge on the forehead between the eyes, indicating larger sinuses. This feature, called the *jibbah* by the Bedouin, is believed to have helped the horse survive in its dry desert homeland.

The second major Thoroughbred breed is the English Thoroughbred, which is renowned for being a fast racehorse. The great galloping strides of these racehorses can be seen on major racetracks all over the world. English Thoroughbreds are also known for their great versatility; they are successful in dressage, show jumping, and other sports events, and are also used to refine warmblood breeds. Heavy workhorses belonging to farmers were bred with English Thoroughbred racehorses to create leaner, sportier breeds.

❭ To Whom Are Thoroughbreds Suited?

Arabian horses are considered especially beautiful and noble, and they are also particularly talented and people-oriented horses. Although Arabians are mainly bred for show purposes, they are also hardy and versatile riding horses. Arabians are successful in dressage and other Western events, particularly the pleasure event. Their flowing movements make them relatively easy to ride. For those who are specifically seeking a cutting horse, trained to separate a cow from its herd, a quarter horse would probably be the best option.

Arabian horses also make up the majority of starting—and winning—horses for endurance races. These events are between sixteen and one hundred miles long. During the longer races, Arabians repeatedly prove they are the true endurance professionals and can gallop for hours at a relaxed pace without showing any sign of exhaustion. For those seeking a fast horse with endurance and a people-oriented and sensitive personality, an Arabian horse is the best option. Those who only want a gentle ride on a horse once a week with a long rein, and those who are a bit scared or uncertain, would not be suited to an Arabian. A rider's fear or anxiety can be sensed by the horse and cause an underutilized Arabian to be nervous and very restless.

An English Thoroughbred is almost certainly equally sensitive, but unlike most Arabian horses, they are better suited to equestrian sport disciplines. The flowing movements of the small Arabian are not sufficient for the demands of athletic riders; the English Thoroughbred riding style is more expansive and with very powerful movements. The majority of these horses are incredibly versatile. English Thoroughbreds are also more spirited than other warmbloods. Therefore, the English Thoroughbred can sometimes be too lively for dressage, show jumping, or tournaments requiring versatility. Moreover, the spectacular movements required for classical dressage may not necessarily be a Thoroughbred's speciality. However, Thoroughbreds are very attentive and quick to learn.

⌃ Arabians are renowned for their beauty.

‹ Arabians are sensitive and tend to have a good bond with their humans.

45

Arabian

Height: 57–61 inches

Color: all colors

Origin: from the Arabian Peninsula to Persia, North Africa

An Arabian horse is characterized by its concave head profile.

Arabian horses are bred all over the world and are considered to be the epitome of equine beauty. The noblest of all the Arabians is the purebred Asil, which descended from horses of the Bedouin people. A typical characteristic of the Arabian is its concave, or "dished," side profile. Their large eyes give them a gentle appearance. Arabian horses come in all colors except pinto, which does not occur naturally in purebred Arabians. However, some breeders attempt to breed pintos with a high proportion of Arabian blood.

Arabians were originally used as perennial warhorses. Today, they are known for their speed and endurance, which is why they are often seen participating in endurance races. These horses, with their graceful gallop, can cover up to one hundred miles per day. Numerous Arabian horses have been successful in Western sporting events, primarily the pleasure discipline. Arabians are not only known for their perseverance, but they are also known for their gentle temperament. They are very friendly and tend to form close bonds with their owners. It is said that long ago, the Bedouin shared their tents with their horses. Life in the desert ensured a rigorous natural selection process: not only the gentlest horses survived but also the healthiest and most persevering.

Arabians need regular exercise
so they do not become
hyperactive and unbalanced.

Anglo-Arabian

Height: 61–65 inches

Color: chestnut, brown, and white

Origin: France

Anglo-Arabians were used in the French Army as cavalry horses.

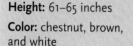

Anglo-Arabians have ideal proportions and move exceptionally well.

Anglo-Arabians originated from a crossing between English Thoroughbreds and Arabian horses in 1835. The aim was to combine the best possible characteristics of each breed to create a noble and very fast sport horse.

The resulting Anglo-Arabian had the noble head of the Thoroughbred, a long neck, and sloping shoulders.

They have a narrow barrel (rib cage) and a slightly sloping croup. Although the legs are never perfectly straight, this breed is capable of long galloping strides and has an outstanding jumping ability. The breeding of Anglo-Arabians is not uniform. The horses can be roughly separated into two groups: the primordial Anglo-Arabian type is a smaller racehorse, while the second type is larger and resembles a noble warmblood horse. The number of original Anglo-Arabs that carry a high proportion of Arabian Thoroughbred blood has decreased because the sport horse is now in high demand. French Anglo-Arabian breeding of riding and sport horses takes place in the city of Pompadour, famous for its stud farm, the Pompadour National Anglo-Arab Stud, headquarters of the French National Stud. Racehorses are bred in the Pau area of France.

English Thoroughbred

Height: 59–67 inches

Color: all colors, mostly brown and chestnut

Origin: England

Three stallions, a Byerley Turk, a Darley Arabian, and a Godolphin Barb, are considered to be the sires of the modern Thoroughbred breed.

High speed: English Thoroughbreds are particularly quick.

English Thoroughbreds have been bred in England since the seventeenth century. They are renowned for their success in horse racing. They are mostly brown or chestnut colored; white or black horses are less common. They are separated into three different groups: steepler (jumping), flyer (sprinter), and stayer (long distance type). English Thoroughbreds are now bred worldwide. A special rule for registering Thoroughbreds is a name can only be used once—and it is not easy finding a truly unique name!

Thoroughbreds are also used to refine other horse breeds and have helped to create virtually all warmblood breeds. In tournaments, they display their true versatility.

Shagya Arabian

Height: 59–63 inches
Color: usually white
Origin: Hungary

Shagya Arabians have existed for more than two hundred years, or to be more precise, since 1789.

Most Shagyas are white.

The Shagya is the "big brother" of the Thoroughbred Arabian. It is slightly larger and stronger, but the oriental influence is clearly visible. As with the Arabians, the Shagyas have a slightly concave head, or "dished profile." Shagya are relatively short horses. They have steep, not particularly long shoulders leading to a short back and ending in a slightly sloping croup with a high-set tail.

Shagyas were bred in the Hungarian state of Bábolna. Lipizzaner, Kladruber, and Hungarian-Moldavian horses were crossed with Thoroughbred Arabians to create the Shagya breed. Patriarchs of the Shagya Arabian stallions are the studs Shagya, Siglavy, Gazlan, and Dahoman O'Bajan. The Shagya horses from Bábolna were ideal horses for the cavalry and were initially used as driving horses and for light work. They were originally referred to as the Arabic breed.

Shagya Arabian horses often have a talent for jumping and dressage.

Hispano-Árabe

Height: 61–65 inches

Color: usually brown, white, and chestnut

Origin: Spain

The Hispano-Árabe, or Spanish Arabian, and other such crossings have almost completely wiped out the pure Andalusian breed.

Breeders of Hispano-Árabes aim to mix the best characteristics of both Arabian and Spanish horses.

The Hispano-Árabe breed is a result of crossing Spanish horses, such as Andalusians, with Arabians or Anglo-Arabians. This crossing created an extremely popular and unusually elegant horse, whose Arabian features are clearly recognizable, mainly from the shape of the head. Their combination of strength and Arabian influence is considered particularly valuable. They are stronger than purebred Arabians but lighter than purebred Spanish horses. Typical Iberian features, such as a convex profile or the high knee action, are usually not clearly present. Hispano-Árabe horses were formerly used by the military and were bred specifically from the mid-nineteenth century onward. By the early twentieth century, they were widespread. Today, Hispano-Árabes have become less common in Spain, and the stallions are mainly used to refine other horse breeds.

Tersk

Height: 59–63 inches

Color: usually white or gray, black or red roan; chestnut is rare

Origin: North Caucasus (Russia)

Tersk horses are a new Russian breed.

Tersk horses are a Russian breed very similar to Arabian horses. They are somewhat larger than the Arabian horse but have inherited the same small head as well as the small ears and large eyes. Their overall appearance strongly resembles that of an Arabian. The Tersk horse has very good endurance and a particularly pronounced canter. As with Arabians, Tersks are most commonly gray. Tersks were bred on the Tersk stud farm in the North Caucasus with the aim of developing a breed similar to the Arabian racehorse. The basis of the breed was the Streletzker horse, which originated from Ukrainian indigenous mares and Oriental stallions.

Streletzkers were bred toward the end of the nineteenth century on the Streletzki stud farm. They were also very similar to Arabian horses but larger, like the Tersk. The unfortunately now-extinct Streletzker was crossed with Arabian Russian Dons, Thoroughbreds, and Shagya Arabians because by the end of the Russian Revolution and civil war, the number of remaining Streletzker horses was too small to continue the breed. The descendants of these crosses from the Streletzker horses were again crossed with Arabians until the Tersk was finally recognized as a breed in its own right in 1948. Tersk horses specialize in flat runs, where they compete against Arabians. Somewhat larger and more compact than Arabian horses, the Tersks are suitable as dressage horses. Nowadays, they can be seen participating in endurance races and also in the circus.

Tersk horses graze in their ideal environment, which has lots of space.

Baroque Horses

< Today, in Lipica, Slovenia, the Lipizzaner herd can be seen on the Karst plateau near Triest.

> The typical convex head profile of the Kladruber is not as obvious in the foal as in the adult horse.

Baroque horses, which include Andalusians, Lipizzaners, and Friesians, among others, are very similar to horses depicted in baroque paintings from the seventeenth and eighteenth centuries. These breeds also have a "baroque" body: a short, broad back with a rounded croup. Other typical features are the high-arched neck; long, thick mane; and a straight-to-convex head profile.

Their build makes these baroque horses particularly well suited to classical dressage. The short back, the upright position, and the spectacular front leg action have predestined these breeds to participate in the art of classical riding. These include such exercises as the piaffe,

a highly collected and cadenced trot; the passage, a slow motion trot; the levade, a movement in which the horse first lowers its body on increasingly bent hocks, then sits on its hind hooves while keeping its forelegs raised and drawn in; and the capriole, a movement in which the horse leaps from the ground, tucks in its front legs, and kicks out with its hind legs. These talents seem to be almost innate in baroque horses.

> To Whom Are Baroque Horses Suited?

Baroque horses are primarily suited for those interested in the art of classical riding. However, one should not make

talent as coach horses. Baroque horses are less suited to long-distance riding. Sublime, soaring kicks are all very well, but keeping up this pace and endurance for long distances at high speeds is not possible for the majority.

◄ Lusitanos are the pride of the Portuguese.

the mistake of believing that these horses are easy to ride; in fact, just the opposite is true! Temperament mixed with strength and an upright position means it is not at all easy to ride a baroque horse.

› Baroque Horses

A well-trained baroque horse is a dream for both riders and spectators, but riding without the necessary knowledge is no more possible than with any other breed—no one would be expected to be able to complete an advanced jumping event with a talented warmblood without the appropriate training. Baroque horses are often very good driving horses. Friesians are especially known for their

Andalusian

Height: 61–64 inches

Color: all colors, usually white

Origin: Spain

The perfect example of classical dressage can be admired at the Royal Andalusian Riding School in Jerez, Spain.

Purebred Andalusians are referred to as PRE, which stands for *pura raza española*, which means "pure Spanish breed." The purest bloodline is the Cartujano (Carthusian), which was bred in the monasteries in southern Spain.

In the Middle Ages, Spanish horse breeds flourished and were in great demand from the European royal courts. They were also ideal warhorses. Andalusians are strong enough to carry an adult male wearing heavy armor. Later, the Andalusians became popular as show and parade horses. Heavily influenced by Berbers, Andalusians are rather short, squat horses with strong necks. The breed has a high front leg action, an upright position, and very impressive movements. Spanish horses have influenced many other fine breeds; the influence of the Andalusian breed can be clearly seen in the Lipizzaner, Kladruber, Frederiksborger, and Friesian.

Berber

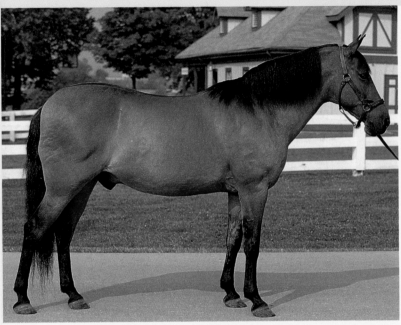

Height: 59–63 inches

Color: commonly white; also brown, chestnut, and black

Origin: North Africa

There are only a few purebred Berbers left; many Arabians and Berbers have been crossbred together.

Berber horses are named after the Berber people, the original inhabitants of North Africa. There, they were coveted warhorses. In peacetime, they were used for training for the traditional equestrian performance in Morrocco called fantasia. Fantasia is inspired by historical wartime attacks of Berber riders and is considered a cultural art and a form of martial art. It also symbolizes a strong relationship between the man and the horse and is highly steeped in tradition.

The medium-sized Berber usually has a lightly convex profile and bears a stronger resemblance to the Iberian horse than the Arabian. The Berber has a short back and is very compact. Berbers have expansive movements with high knee action and are sure footed, quick, and agile.

The suitability of the Berbers for classical dressage made them popular with the cavalry captains in Renaissance and Baroque times and promoted this breed as a refiner of many other horse breeds in Europe from then on.

The Arabian Berber emerged from a crossing of both breeds. It is between fifty-nine and sixty-three inches tall and usually has softer movements than the Berber. Some Arabian Berbers show a talent for tölt, which often seems to be innate. Unlike the purebred Berber, Arabian Berbers often participate in endurance races.

57

Friesian

Height: mares 59 inches, stallions more than 63 inches

Color: black

Origin: West Friesland, Netherlands

Friesians are always black; only a small white star is permitted.

A typical characteristic of the Friesian is its long, wavy mane.

Friesians have a very high-set neck and are quite large and proud looking. Typical features are the shiny black coat, long mane, and feathering (long hair above the hooves).

Their movements are very flowing, and they have high knee action. They were originally bred for agricultural work. They are somewhere in the middle between a warmblood and a coldblood. The Friesian horse was famous in the Middle Ages as a sport horse for armored knights.

A warrior with full armor weighed up to seven hundred fifty pounds! Being able to bear such a weight requires an immense amount of strength.

Friesians were bred over the centuries without significant crossbreeding with other breeds; they remain relatively unchanged. However, the fact that they have so little foreign blood in them is a disadvantage because they have a fairly low population and a high proportion of inbreeding. Since the nineteenth century, Friesians have been coveted driving horses but were also used for the cavalry. They also do very well in the circus and are known to have a docile nature. Friesians have seen a surge in popularity in recent years due to their spectacular appearances in various shows. They are also often used for riding.

∧ Friesians are very impressive; they often appear to be larger than they really are.

< Driving seems to be an innate skill for Friesians.

59

Kladruber

Height: about 66 inches

Color: white, black

Origin: Czech Republic

Kladrubers were used as carriage horses for kings.

In 1579 in Bohemia (now the Czech Republic), the Kladruber stud farm was founded, making it the oldest, largest stud farm in the world. In 1995, this stud farm and the horses were declared a national cultural monument of the Czech Republic. The Kladruber horses are excellent driving horses, and their imposing appearance ensured they were highly sought after as carriage horses for nobility.

The white and black horses' baroque origins are clear to see. The white horses originated from an Italian stallion named Pepoli, whose famous son Imperatore founded the white lineage of this breed. The black lineage can be traced back to an Italian stallion named Sacramoso, born in Salzburg. More recently, a Friesian stallion was used to refine this breed. The white Kladrubers were traditionally the carriage horses of the kings, while the black horses were used by ecclesiastical (church) rulers. At the beginning of the twentieth century, after the decline of the Czech monarchy, public interest in Kladrubers waned. They became so rare that they were eventually protected by the United Nations.

Sadly, Kladruber foals have become very rare.

Knabstrupper

The most famous Knabstrupper is fictional children's book character Pippi Longstocking's horse.

The Knabstrupper of the original baroque type horse is rare today. Each horse is very different, but they all have leopard markings. These come in different types: the pelmet leopard (mostly dark with a spotted white section), the snowflake leopard (white spots on a dark coat), and—the best known variant—the full leopard, a polka-dot pattern on a white coat. White and solid colored horses are uncommon. Many Knabstruppers have slightly convex heads and long backs. These colorful horses are closely related to Frederiksborgers. They are considered to be extremely intelligent, so when they are underutilized, they can be difficult to manage.

Over time, different breeds were crossed with the Knabstrupper, so the original type has become increasingly rare. Today, some adventurous mixtures without papers are sold as Knabstruppers. Horses with 90 percent foreign blood are permitted in Denmark by the studbook. The Knabstrupper faces extinction, despite efforts made since 1970 to preserve the baroque breed.

Each horse is very special. The spots of the Knabstrupper are truly unique.

Lipizzaner

Height: 58–62 inches

Color: usually white

Origin: Slovenia

Lipizzaners are world famous for their demonstrations at the Spanish Riding School in Vienna, Austria.

Lipizzaners come from Lipica, Slovenia. The stud farm was founded in 1585, but the horses endured several wartime relocations that prevented extinction of the breed. Lipizzaners are also bred on a stud farm in Piber, Austria, and are used by the Spanish Riding School in Vienna, where they perform classical dressage demonstrations. These peformances include not only riding exercises but also a segment called the "airs above the ground." These are the spectacular leaps and maneuvers once used by soldiers to defend themselves on the battlefield, which are now preserved as equestrian art. When you see the Lipizzaners perform, it is like stepping back four hundred years and viewing one of the greatest equine ballets in history. The Lipizzaners are renowned for baroque dressage but there are many successful driving horses as well.

Lipizzaners are almost exclusively white; brown or black horses are rare. The influence of the Iberian horses can be clearly seen in the Lipizzaner. Lipizzaners have slightly convex heads; powerful, high upright necks; and high knee action.

The epitome of classical dressage: a Lipizzaner in Vienna

Lusitano

Height: 59–63 inches
Color: all colors
Origin: Portugal

The Altér Real is a special type of Lusitano.

Lusitanos are very similar to Andalusians. The breed was officially recognized in 1942 as an independent breed. Unlike Anadalusians, however, Lusitanos have stayed closer to their original type. They were not crossed with Arabian horses as often as the Andalusians were; therefore, they have a more convex head profile. Lusitanos are bred on a stud farm in Coudelaria in southern Portugal.

Lusitanos are often white, brown, or dun but come in all other colors. They are very well suited to bullfighting and classical dressage and so have made a name for themselves in Europe. The exemplary curved neck and gently sloping croup are ideal conditions for riding in an upright position. Lusitanos are therefore immensely popular with baroque horse fans.

A beautiful Lusitano in full show gear

63

Coldbloods

< Unfortunately, many coldbloods have docked tails.

> Nowadays, many coldbloods are used to pull carts for tourists.

Coldbloods are heavy draft horses and make very strong workhorses. Do not let the term *coldblood* fool you: their blood or body temperature is not any colder than those of other horses. It is only their temperament that is somewhat cooler; they are quiet, thoughtful, and less hot tempered than Thoroughbreds, for example.

Some heavy draft horse breeds can weigh up to twenty-two hundred pounds. Today, they are unfortunately only rarely needed in the fields to pull the plow, to shift logs, or to pull heavy carriages, so they are now fairly rare.

> To Whom Are Coldbloods Suited?

Coldbloods are suitable for any work in the agricultural and forestry area that must be carried out in an ecologically sustainable way, for example, shifting logs, plowing fields, or moving heavy loads. Since this work can be carried out more quickly using machinery, coldbloods are no longer really needed. However, they are still used for alternative methods of farming and forestry. Coldbloods are capable of carrying out hard, heavy work. They pull brewery carriages and tourist carts. Their smooth, calm movement and reliability mean that coldbloods also

make ideal leisure horses. They have proved their skills and reliability, not just pulling carts but also as riding horses. Their specialty is not a rapid, persistent gallop but rather a quieter, more diligent walk or trot. They are not suited to long distances.

‹ Draft horses are no longer bred very often. Many breeds are threatened with extinction.

Ardennes

Height: 61–64 inches

Color: brown, wire-haired chestnut, white

Origin: Belgium and France

Some Ardennes horses can weigh more than twenty-two hundred pounds.

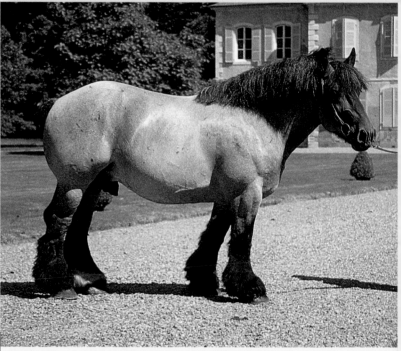

The Ardennes breed originates from the Solutré horse from the Stone Age. This horse breed was used in Ardennes in the Roman legions, as well as in the Napoleon artillery, and had an average weight of 1,764 to 2,205 pounds.

Arabian Thoroughbreds were used to refine the breed, and it has therefore inherited the Arabian's remarkable stamina.

The modern Ardennes is very similar to the Belgian. It is a relatively small, medium-weight, hardworking draft horse. In Sweden, this breed is still used to move logs; the small, noble Ardennes type is well established there. As in Belgium and France, the original duties of this breed in the Ardennes Forest—agriculture, forestry, and work for the army—are now carried out by machines, so Ardennes are mainly bred for meat. Therefore, the heavier, stronger Ardennes is more popular, while the smaller Arabian type is slowly dying out.

Belgian Draft Horse

Height: 64–68 inches

Color: red roan with black points, chestnut

Origin: Belgium

Belgian drafts are also known as Brabant horses.

Belgian draft horses can weigh up to a ton or more. Their size and weight are impressive for a coldblood breed. The docked tail emphasises the broad, split croup.

The Belgians are closely related to the Ardennes breed and like them, they have a history of being highly valued warhorses and workhorses in agriculture. Unfortunately, the Belgian, which belongs to the heaviest horse breeds in the world, is now almost exclusively bred for meat. Only a small amount of horse fans use the Belgians for alternative methods of forestry and agriculture or for brewery cart rides. Because Belgians are not suitable for tournaments, this breed, which has been around since Roman times, has a very uncertain future. They are rarely bred.

Boulonnais

Height: 61–63 inches

Color: white, chestnut, and brown

Origin: France

Boulonnais are regarded by many as being the most beautiful coldblood horses of all.

The Boulonnais is an elegant horse, despite its size and weight. The Oriental influence can be seen in the head profile and its movements are very light and flowing. The frequent occurrence of the white horses in this French coldblood breed is due to their Arabian heritage. The breed is considered to be a successful combination of grace and strength.

Originally, there were two types of these attractive horses: a light type with sweeping, energetic trot that was used by fishermen on the coast, and the heavier type that was able to pull heavy loads. The heavy Boulonnais were used to uncouple railway wagons, which is why they were also known as "Wagonniers." The lighter type is now almost extinct. Although the Boulonnais is still used in agriculture, particularly on small holdings, it is often bred for meat.

Breton

Height: 61–64 inches

Color: chestnut, white, red roan, black

Origin: Brittany, France

Breton horses can weigh up to 1,984 pounds.

Bretons originated in Brittany, France, where these workhorses were bred for centuries. They were formerly known as Roussins or Sommiers. Today, there are two types of Bretons: the light roadster, which was refined by Norfolk and Hackney horses, called Postier Bretons, and the heavier type, which was crossed with Percherons, Ardennes, and Boulonnais. The heavier Breton is called the Trait Breton and is the most numerous of the Bretons, also because it is used for meat. A faster, lighter type, which was a result of crossing with Arabians and Thoroughbreds, became the Selle Français breed and no longer exists as the Breton type. Bretons are considered particularly quiet, strong, and good natured, with energetic, light movements. Although they can weigh close to two thousand pounds, Bretons are only about sixty-four inches tall.

Clydesdale

Height: 65–68 inches

Color: all colors, often brown and white

Origin: Scotland

Clydesdale horses have large, symmetrical markings and coarse fur.

A typical characteristic of the Clydesdale is the white markings on the head and legs; these markings are very similar to those of the shire horse.

The Clydesdale is a traditional Scottish workhorse. It is slightly lighter than the shire horse but is renowned for its incredibly hardworking nature. During a benchmark test in Versailles, France, shortly before the beginning of the twentieth century, a team of two Clydesdales performed just as well as the other teams with three horses. It surpassed the abilities of proven draft horses such as Percherons and Boulonnais. Clydesdales, like all classical workhorses, have decreased in number, mainly due to the fact that the law in the United Kingdom effectively forbids the export of live animals for slaughter. Thus we see the Scottish draft horses today only rarely as representative draft horses in carriage pulling competitions. The huge, powerful Clydesdales fare particularly well at this. These peaceful coldbloods make an impression with their high, upright position and high-set necks. They are usually black, dark brown, or brown. Chestnuts are undesirable. Large markings are a typical feature of this breed.

Freiberger

Height: 59 inches
Color: brown, chestnut
Origin: Jura, west Switzerland

Freibergers are used by the Swiss army.

Freibergers are the only primitive Swiss breed in existence and come from the high plateau of the Jura Mountains. A Freiberger weighs between 1,213 and 1,433 pounds and is a compact, medium-sized horse. A relatively short neck and short legs characterize the appearance of this horse, which was bred in the Swiss mountains over many centuries. Freibergers are light draft horses used today to work in the fields and forests. They are very good natured, hardy in attitude, and suitable for riding as well as driving. But they also now have a good reputation as therapy horses, disability sport horses, and vaulting horses. In their homeland, they are bred as sport horses and for meat.

Freibergers are very energetic movers, so they have become increasingly popular in recent years.

71

Jutland

Height: 61–64 inches

Color: chestnut

Origin: Denmark

Jutlands are also known as Jutes or Jydsks.

The Jutland breed can be traced back to the twelfth century when horses were used for battles. Today, Jutlands

are powerful, sturdy workhorses with rugged, compact heads. They have long, light-colored manes. An efficient, seemingly inexhaustible trot affords these chestnut-colored horses plenty of driving power. Because of this power and also their lively yet pleasant natures, Jutlands are very popular as carriage horses. They have been used as brewery horses—usually in a team of four—since 1928 for a large brewery in Copenhagen, Denmark.

Jutlands weigh between 1,433 and 1,874 pounds. They are a little heavier than their close relatives, the Schleswig horses, and are also bred for meat. This practice has probably saved them from extinction. Originally, Jutlands were brown, dark brown, and black, but these colors are rare in the Jutland today.

Noriker

Height: 61–67 inches

Color: all colors, including pinto and marshmallow

Origin: Austria

The marshmallow color is a gray-white color with a darker head.

Norikers have probably been around for more than two thousand years. The name of these moderately heavy draft horses was derived from the former Roman province of Noricum, which, roughly speaking, is now present-day Austria and Bavaria. In the region of Pinzgau, southwest of Salzburg, in 1565, the first studbook was created for breeding control. The Noriker breed was therefore also called the Pinzgauer. Today, in the various breeding regions, they tend to have different characteristics. It is emphasized, however, that all Norikers should have a heavy head with a slightly convex nose profile. They are usually brown or chestnut in color, as well as leopard, pinto, and marshmallow, which for some is the preferred color and thus bred specifically.

Originally used as workhorses in the Alps, Norikers are now used as riding and driving horses. The more colorful horses are used in the circus and for pulling brewery wagons or traditional carriages for tourists.

Percheron

Height: 63–67 inches

Color: white and black

Origin: France

Percherons were crossed with Arabian horses.

The Percheron exhibits the elegance of an Arabian and the strength of a coldblood. Typical features are the white color, the noble head with wide forehead and slightly concave profile, sure-footedness, and lack of feathering on the lower legs.

Percherons come from an area called Le Perche, southwest of Paris. They were used to transport knights and were repeatedly crossed with Arabians. This created elegant coldbloods that were very popular because, among other reasons, in contrast to other coldbloods, they have a relatively small amount of feathering on the lower legs. Feathering traps moisture and can cause skin diseases.

The Percheron has a varied history: he was the horse of the warrior and the peasants, pulled carriages as well as plows, and was also used as a riding horse. Percherons are sturdy and clever with a placid temperament. Although he carries a lot of Arabian blood, the Percheron breed never became any lighter over

time. The most powerful stallion ever known was the Percheron named Dr. Le Gear, who was 84 inches tall and weighed 3,025 pounds.

Percherons are considered to be good natured, as well as very hardworking, but are sometimes a little too motivated. This is where their Arabian temperament comes into play. Unfortunately, they are now hardly used as driving and workhorses but mostly bred for meat. Therefore, the breed has deteriorated because more emphasis is put on a high weight rather than healthy joints. However, breeders are now campaigning to preserve the traditional draft horse breeds.

^ A Percheron at work. At the turn of the century, Percherons were the most valued draft horses in France. In addition to being used in agriculture and the artillery, the white draft horses were used to pull stagecoaches. Their bright color made them more visible in the dark.

< Black Percherons still exist.

75

Black Forest Horse

Height: 57–60 inches

Color: dark chestnut with a long flaxen mane

Origin: the Black Forest in Germany

Black Forest horses weigh about eleven hundred pounds.

Black Forest horses are a very attractive dark chestnut color.

Black Forest horses, as their name suggests, originate from the Black Forest in Germany. There, they are traditionally bred in a rather uniform type of small, powerful draft horse. All Black Forest horses are dark chestnut with a long flaxen mane. The mane frames a fine head, a compact body, and a medium-length neck. These features combine to create an attractive workhorse that is also bred as a show horse. This is in part due to their good-natured, lively temperament and their very impressive movements.

The Black Forest horses were always bred according to agility and frugality rather than their weight. They have an average weight of eleven hundred pounds, which is relatively light for a coldblood breed.

Black Forest horses are among the old workhorse breeds. In the seventeenth century, they were used for forestry and field work. Since 1896, they have been maintained by their own breeding association. In the 1950s and 1960s, the number of Black Forest horses decreased significantly—as with

Black Forest horses are also bred in Alb, Swabia.

the other heavy horse breeds—and they had to be included on the list of endangered breeds of farm animals. The establishment of stud farms in Baden-Württemberg and Marbach and the increase of tourism in the Black Forest have seen their numbers rise once again.

Many Black Forest horses are bred as show horses.

Schleswiger

Height: about 62 inches

Color: chestnut with a lighter-colored mane

Origin: Schleswig-Holstein, Germany

Schleswigers were nearly extinct.

Schleswigers are traditional workhorses; their driving talent seems to be innate.

The Schleswiger is a relatively new breed. Toward the end of the nineteenth century, this breed was created by crossing various different draft horses. Jutland horses from Denmark were strongly involved in creating the breed. Schleswigers are particularly widespread in Schleswig-Holstein but rarely seen in other parts of Germany. There was once a large number of Schleswigers in Lower Saxony.

The Schleswiger is a medium-sized horse of moderate weight. The powerful, capable workhorse is very tolerant and—due to its medium size—also quite agile. Schleswigers are considered to be very personable and persistent. Most Schleswigers are chestnut colored. Unfortunately, they are now threatened with extinction. In 1949, there were approximately twenty-five thousand mares and four hundred and fifty stallions; however, by 1976, due to the lack of demand for working horses, this number had declined to thirty-six mares and five stallions. Today, efforts are being intensified again to preserve these hardworking draft horses. Schleswigers are also used to shift logs and are used as workhorses in tree nurseries.

Shire Horse

Height: 67–77 inches

Color: black, white, and brown

Origin: England

Shire horses are the largest horses in the world.

At more than seventy-five inches tall, shires are giant, even for horses. The head is long and slender, with large eyes and a slightly arched, relatively long neck. They have deep, wide shoulders; wide chests; short, muscular backs; and long, wide hindquarters. There is not too much feathering on the legs, and the hair is fine, straight, and silky. They also have high leg action, and this, combined with the high-set neck, makes them quite similar to Friesian horses. Friesian mares were used to refine this breed. Shire horses are considered to be particularly good natured.

Shire horses were originally bred as warhorses that were able to carry knights wearing heavy armor, then later primarily used as carriage horses. Today, depictions of shire horses can still be seen on the coat of arms of many English pubs or breweries. Without large breweries and some rural breeders, shire horses would probably be extinct. These gentle giants are world famous. People cannot fail to be impressed by their handsome appearance.

The beautiful shire horse is a proud symbol of English heritage.

Small Horses and Ponies

< There are various di
sizes of Welsh ponies,
subdivided into differe
categories.

> Falabellas are parti
small and are not bred
riding horses.

>> Ponies are great
beginner horses and a
not just for children.

All ponies are small horses, but not all small horses are ponies. Generally, ponies are small horses that are less than fifty-eight inches tall, but depending on context, a pony may be a horse that is under a certain height at the withers, or a small horse with a specific (gentle) temperament. Arabian horses, for example, are only fifty-seven to sixty-one inches tall but are classified as Thoroughbreds. Typical ponies and small horses include the Connemara and Gypsy Vanner from Ireland; Dartmoor ponies and Welsh ponies from England; Fjord horses, originally from Norway; Haflingers; and Icelandic horses.

The latter are, however, gaited horses—a description of these horses can be found in the next chapter.

Many of the actual pony breeds are in fact taller than fifty-eight inches: Haflingers and Gypsy Vanners are sometimes larger.

> To Whom Are Ponies Suited?

Pony breeds are very diverse, so there is a pony suited to every personal preference or requirement. Smaller, more docile ponies often make excellent riding horses for children and adolescents. Children who are not big enough to ride a warmblood horse can learn to ride on ponies. Young riders often celebrate their first successes at equestrian events with their ponies. German riding ponies are particularly suited to dressage and jumping events. Very similar in appearance to the athletic warmbloods, these smaller relatives win many prizes in pony-sport competitions. However, temperamental sport ponies require experienced riders.

In principle, ponies, just like horses, have a healthy dose of

Among the many pony and small horse breeds are some very good driving horses, for example, the miniature Shetland pony, which is amazingly powerful and a highly agile driving horse.

self-awareness, and should never be used as toys for children. Just as with any horse, they need proper training, their needs must be meet, and they must be given meaningful tasks. The stronger ponies are very good for larger adolescents and adults as well as being suitable as leisure horses. The Haflingers and Norwegian Fjords, for example, are popular riding horses for a variety of equestrian disciplines, from small dressage and jumping events to Western tournaments and short and medium endurance races. These sturdy ponies can do almost anything! Their very balanced temperament also helps uneasy riders to feel more confident.

⌄ Keeping a pony is an ideal way for children to learn all that horse care entails.

Bosnian Mountain Horse

Height: 53–57 inches

Color: mainly brown and dun

Origin: Bosnia

Bosnians are one of the most widespread breeds of mountain horse in the world.

Bosnians were used by people as transport horses long before the Christian era. They are the typical mountain horses of Bosnia and Herzegovina, but they are also widespread in other areas of the Balkans. Bosnians originate from mountainous regions, so they are very sure footed, intelligent, persevering, and have a strong character. These workhorses belonging to farmers were always relatively small, but in recent years they have been bred to be somewhat larger and heavier. They have been crossed with light draft horses in order to increase their size and so obtain a higher price for their meat.

During the Turkish occupation of their homeland (1463–1875), Bosnians were crossed with Arabian horses. The Bosnians inherited their fine head shape from Arabians. From about 1900, the Arabian influence on the breed came to an end because the hybrids were not suitable as packhorses. Since then, Bosnians are mostly purebred, but in recent times there has been some uncontrolled breeding with larger horses. Bosnian mountain horses are considered an endangered breed.

Camargue

Height: 53–59 inches
Color: white
Origin: Camargue, France

Camargue horses live semiwild in Camargue, France.

The Camargue horses live in Camargue, in the South of France—a landscape of swamp and sandy savannah on the Mediterranean. They live among black bulls and are used to herd cattle. To do this, Camargues have to be very fast and agile because the bulls can sometimes be quite aggressive and have long horns.

Camargues are invariably white. They are quite strong and even the smaller ones can carry an adult. Typical features include the slightly convex head profile and sturdy neck. The Iberian or Berber influence can be seen in many of these horses. Due to this influence, Camargue horses are suitable for classic baroque riding, which makes them popular horses for the discerning leisure rider.

In their homeland, Camargues mostly live in herds.

83

Connemara

Height: 55–58 inches

Color: usually white and dun; black, brown, or chestnut are rare

Origin: West of Ireland

From about 1950, the Connemaras were crossed with Thoroughbreds, Arabians, and Irish draft horses.

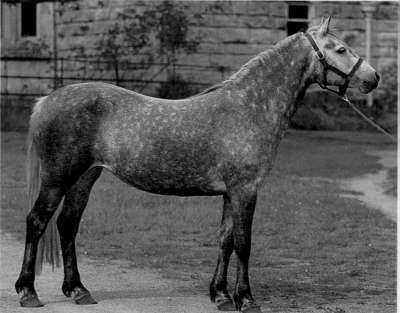

The Connemara ponies come from Connemara, a hilly and rocky landscape on the Atlantic coast of western Ireland. Over time, they have adapted very well to their arid environment and are particularly frugal. The Connemara has a strong body, and its character is generally highly praised for being quiet and reliable. The Connemara has a lovely, expressive face; a long neck; and a good saddle position. Their movements are energetic and expansive, so they are also suitable for tournaments. Connemara ponies are now the most popular and powerful adult and children's riding ponies and are also well known for their jumping abilities.

Originally, the typical Connemara mountain horses of farmers were used as packhorses and riding horses. They are very sure footed, so they are suitable for trail rides.

Dales Pony

Height: about 58 inches

Color: mostly black and black-brown

Origin: England

The Dales pony is closely related to the Fell pony.

The roots of Dales and Fell ponies can be traced back to Celtic ponies from Galloway in Scotland. Both are very strong pony breeds that can carry a large amount of weight. They were initially used as transport horses between the mines and the port cities and also commonly used as packhorses. Since both pony breeds are good trotters and also sure footed, they make very good riding horses. In the nineteenth century, Dales mares were crossed with a Welsh cob stallion called Comet, who founded one of the main lines that can be traced back today. They were later crossed with numerous Clydesdales but unfortunately have a decreased trotting ability and have lost their hardiness.

In 1917, the Dales pony breed was given its own studbook and was therefore recognized as an independent breed. In about 1950, they nevertheless almost became extinct, as motorization of agriculture and transportation made these ponies unnecessary.

Above: With their black fur and feathered fetlocks, the Dales ponies are strongly reminiscent of the Dutch Friesian. Indeed, a Friesian influence is suspected at the time of the Roman rule in Britain. The Romans loved the vigorous black horses and used them frequently during battle.

Left: Dales ponies turn heads at every tournament.

85

Dartmoor Pony

Height: 49 inches

Color: all colors except pinto

Origin: England

Dartmoor ponies were formerly used in the mining industry.

Dartmoor ponies are from the moors and heathlands of Dartmoor Forest in the southwest of England. Only very strong animals can survive the hard life on the moors; therefore, the Dartmoor ponies are very tough. Dartmoor ponies have been crossbred with countless other breeds, including Thoroughbreds, Hackneys, and cobs. Only the most hardy horses of these breeds were used for crossbreeding with Dartmoor ponies.

The short, stout ponies were perfectly suited to mining. Shetland ponies were often crossed with Dartmoor ponies to make them even smaller and so more suited to mining work. This meant the original Dartmoor ponies almost died out. The old breed, said to have existed since about 1012, was rescued by a private breeding association in 1899.

Since then, Dartmoor ponies, which are very good with children, have been specifically bred for their tremendous jumping abilities. Their beautiful gait has also made them popular with adult riders, who have found them to be hardworking driving horses.

The establishment of a training area for the military in Dartmoor led to a reduction in the number of ponies in their homeland. However, they continue to be bred outside of this area and also on the European continent.

Exmoor Pony

Height: 49 inches

Color: dark dun or dark brown, no markings

Origin: England

The pale muzzle is a typical feature of the Exmoor pony.

Exmoor ponies are small dun or dark brown ponies with pale muzzles. This breed is threatened with extinction. They are thought to be descendants of Celtic ponies, and their history goes as far back as the Bronze Age. The numbers of Exmoor ponies were threatened during World War II, when many ponies were simply slaughtered. Although breeders have been trying to preserve the breed since then, it is still at risk.

Originally used as riding horses and packhorses by farmers on the moors, and later as carriage horses by farmers and traders, Exmoor ponies are extremely bright, hardworking, and noble but also unusually strong: an adult Exmoor pony can bear the weight of a heavy adult for an entire day of riding. They are also known for their good health and longevity. They often live to the age of thirty and longer, and a lame Exmoor pony is a very rare sight.

These little ponies are fairly temperamental and are not ideal for children nor beginner riders, as they are usually too intelligent and will take advantage of the weakness of an inexperienced rider.

German Riding Pony

Height: 54–58 inches
Color: all colors
Origin: Germany

The idea of a "sport pony" is actually an English invention.

Riding ponies have attractive faces.

The German riding pony is basically a miniature warmblood, suitable for children and adolescents. As a sport pony, it was bred for the disciplines of dressage, jumping, and eventing. Eventing, a relatively new discipline, began in about 1975. Dülmen wild horses, as well as Welsh ponies, Arabians, Anglo-Arabians, Thoroughbreds, and other warmbloods were crossed. The aim was to develop a British breed of "riding pony" that would also be suitable for equestrian tournaments. Soon after that, in Germany, a highly successful German riding pony was developed.

As so many different breeds were crossed to create this pony, they come in all colors: brown, chestnut, black, and white are the most common. German riding ponies and warmbloods are only differentiated by their size in tournaments. They are more similar to warmbloods than other pony breeds, such as Haflingers or Norwegian Fjords. The athleticism and the high proportion of Thoroughbred blood comes at a price, however: German riding ponies are very sensitive and are not suitable for uncertain riders or beginners.

Riding ponies, like warmbloods, are suited to classic tournament disciplines, as they are all-terrain horses.

Dülmen Wild Horse

Height: 51–57 inches

Color: mainly dun

Origin: Germany

Dülmen wild horses live in the Merfeld Marsh with almost no human intervention.

Intelligent and very hardy, a Dülmen can learn almost anything.

Dülmen wild horses are all horses that are born in the wild in Merfeld Marsh in Germany. Horses born in captivity and not in this herd are known only as Dülmens because they are not wild horses. Originally, there were several stud farms in Germany for wild horses. Dülmen wild horses survived the abolition of wild stud farms because in 1850, the Duke of Croy ensured that some twenty horses were kept in an enclosure where they could continue to breed. All other wild stud farms no longer exist in Germany. Dülmen wild horses were mentioned in documents dating back to 1316 and are able to survive without human intervention. However, in very harsh winters, they are given extra food. Humans only really intervene once a year; at the end of May, the young stallions are separated from the herd and take part in a folk festival auction. The person who ends up owning the Dülmen at the auction will take home a hardy, healthy, and forgiving family horse. Dülmen wild horses come in all shades of gray and dun, usually without any white markings, and are suitable as riding, driving, and endurance horses.

Falabella Miniature Horse

Height: up to 29.5 inches

Color: all colors

Origin: South America

These horses are bred purely for fun; they are not suitable as driving or riding horses.

The Falabella is an inbred miniature horse that often has a poor physique. The head is usually quite large, the withers rather unpronounced, and a short back leads to a steeply falling croup and a deep-set tail. Falabellas often have weak joints, malformed limbs, and extremely small hooves. They are usually very friendly and are also said to be intelligent, capable of learning, and have a great longevity.

Falabellas are purely a fashion breed. They are named after Juan Falabella, the ranch owner who developed the breed near Buenos Aires, Argentina. The breed is a result of a cross between Shetland ponies and young Thoroughbreds.

Falabellas are selected according to appearance, not ability; they are not suited as driving or riding horses. Nevertheless, Falabellas are known and loved both in Europe and in the United States. They are mostly bred for pure pleasure; however, they are occasionally trained as guide horses for the blind, similar to guide dogs.

Galiceño Pony

Height: 49–54 inches

Color: brown, dun, chestnut, some are wirehaired

Origin: Mexico

This breed was named after its ancestors from Galicia, Spain.

Galiceños are thought to have originated from the horses that Spanish conquerors left behind in the Americas. Their name indicates that they most likely descended from Galician horses.

Accordingly, Galiceños have a similarity to Spanish horses. The Galiceño has a noble head, a lightly convex nose profile, and a fairly high-set neck with very upright head position. Their movements are like those of the Iberians, with high leg action. For this reason, they often tend to make good riding horses.

The Galiceños often appear smaller than their large Iberian relatives, which in many cases was a consequence of lack of food. They are quiet and reliable, which is why they are also used as horses for children and adolescents. They have a talent for jumping, so they do fairly well in horse shows. But they are also successful workhorses in everyday life: the vaqueros (Mexican cowboys) value the "cow sense" of the Galiceños. "Cow sense" refers to a horse's ability to herd cattle.

Fjord Horse

Height: 54–58 inches

Color: dun

Origin: Norway

The white mane tipped with black is an instantly recognizable feature of this breed.

The Norwegian Fjord's coat becomes heavy and thick in the winter.

The Fjord horse, also known as the Norwegian or the Fjording, is among the oldest horse breeds in Europe. The home of this dun horse with the characteristic black and white mane is the mountainous region of western Norway; this rocky area is known for its fjords, which are narrow inlets between cliffs. Fjord horses are reminiscent of a very primitive breed: they strongly resemble the tundra pony from the Ice Age. These powerful small horses often have zebra stripes on their legs. Most Fjord horses have a dorsal stripe on their backs—a long, dark line that runs along the spinal column. White markings are undesirable; however, on the mares, a white star on the forehead is permitted. Fjords are particularly suited as leisure horses for children and adults and have an innate talent as driving horses. They are considered reliable and frugal. The Norwegian Fjord Horse Registry, based in Colorado, recommends that broodmares and stallions undergo performance testing in three disciplines: riding, driving, and draft.

Haflinger

Height: 53–57 inches

Color: chestnut with a lighter mane

Origin: South Tyrol in Italy

Haflingers from Austria and Italy are branded with a firebrand in the shape of an edelweiss, a mountain flower. Horses from Austria and from South Tyrol have the letter "H" in the center of the brand, while horses from all other parts of Italy have the letters "HI."

Haflingers are originally from South Tyrol and were named after their place of origin, the municipality of Hafling. They are hardy all-purpose horses that are easy to care for. The "grandfather" of the Haflingers was the half-Arabian horse El'Bedavi. Although they are pony sized, that is smaller than fifty-eight inches, Haflingers are considered to be particularly strong and versatile, as well as very sure footed and frugal. Haflingers were originally used as packhorses and workhorses in the mountains. The modern Haflingers are lighter and more athletic and are ideal for all types of riding. These chestnut ponies are popular not just as driving horses but also as riding horses for both children and adults. Haflingers can be seen in Western tournaments as well as in smaller dressage, jumping, or endurance events.

Haflingers are one of the most popular breeds for recreational riders.

Highland Pony

Height: about 58 inches

Color: white and dun are the most common; brown and pale fawn are rare

Origin: Scotland and England

Highland ponies and Fjord horses are closely related.

The Highland pony is from the Highlands in Scotland. Its history can be traced right back to the Ice Age. Highland ponies became a registered breed with their own studbook in 1880. In terms of breeding, it is their origin that counts—not their size. Certain colors are undesirable; pinto ponies are not permitted, and except for a small star, markings are generally unwelcome. Highland ponies are a so-called "mountain and moorland" breed; they lived semiwild for generations on moors and in the mountains. The Highland pony has a relatively low leg action. It is suited to riding and driving but can also carry heavy loads. This hardy pony has an even temperament. The thick mane and full tail are characteristic of this breed.

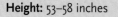

Small Horses and Ponies

Hucul Pony

Height: 53–58 inches

Color: usually brown and dun; rarely black, white, chestnut, and pinto

Origin: Poland

Hucul ponies are descendants of Tarpan ponies.

Hucul ponies are mountain ponies. Their hardiness is legendary: they are extremely frugal and need very little food. But their strength is incredible. It is said that a Hucul can drag a four-hundred-forty-pound deer that has been shot down from the mountain into the valley.

Huculs are not only found in Poland but also in Romania, Slovakia, and are bred in the Czech Republic. Romanian Huculs are slightly larger than Polish Huculs.

Previously, it was believed that Huculs descended from Arabians, perhaps because their head profile is sometimes like that of an Arabian horse. However, it is now thought that they actually originated from the Tarpan ponies in the Russian steppes.

The name of this breed comes from the Hutsul people, the original inhabitants of the Ukraine. Today, the Hucul ponies are quite rare; their numbers have decreased, despite the fact that they make very good riding horses for both adults and children. In Austria, for example, until World War I, Huculs were bred in many areas, but after the war, higher priority was given to the breeding of Haflingers.

98

Konik

Height: about 52 inches
Color: dun
Origin: Poland

The word *Konik* is Polish for "little horse."

Konik ponies are wild ponies, very closely related to the eastern wild horse. The small, compact Konik originates from Poland and lived in the wild right up to the last century. Traditional horse hunting meant their numbers were greatly reduced. Only the creation of a pony reserve and consequent offspring has saved this breed from extinction.

The medium-weight Konik has a straight or slightly concave head and a short neck with a thick mane. The croup curves sharply away and the base of the tail is quite deep set. The Konik is gray-dun or gray-brown with a dark mane. The gray-dun ponies have primitive markings—a dorsal stripe and zebra stripes on the legs.

Koniks are hardworking, hardy, tough, persistent, and are particularly suited to agricultural work. However, they are not always easy to handle.

They are rarely used as riding ponies but instead used to pull small carts. Koniks live in various protected areas, for example, Schleswig-Holstein National Park in Germany, the Geltinger Birk nature reserve on the Baltic, and the Bialowieza National Park in Poland. In Geltinger Birk, a Konik stallion and ten mares were returned to the wild and live on an area of seventy-nine acres with no people or human intervention; the ponies take care of the "landscaping." There has also been a small herd in the German nature reserve of Wöhrdener Loch since 2004.

Lewitzer Pony

Height: 51–58 inches

Color: pinto

Origin: Germany

Lewitzers originate from the Lewitz stud farm in Mecklenburg, Germany.

Lewitzers are the only breed of horse that was created after World War II in East Germany. This breed was officially recognized in 1991. The name comes from Lewitz, a protected landscape in Mecklenburg.

The ponies, which are selected according to their riding abilities, appearance, and pinto coloring, were refined by Trakehner and Thoroughbred breeds.

The Lewitzer is a medium-sized, elegant pony with fast reactions, excellent learning capabilities, and a hardworking nature. They are considered good natured and balanced and are ideal ponies and riding horses for children. Most Lewitzers are black and dark brown pinto, though some are chestnut.

Lewitzers are very good with people, but they can sometimes be temperamental.

100

Mérens

Height: 53–57 inches

Color: black

Origin: Pyrenees and Ariégeois mountains of southern France and northern Spain

Mérens ponies are also known as Ariègeois.

As Mérens are very uniform in type, they look very good working in a team.

Mérens ponies are native to the valley of Ariège, France, next to the Garonne River, whose headwaters lie on the border of Andorra. Today, Mérens are found in the high Alps, Provence Alps, Massif Central, and Cevennes.

Mérens are almost always black, although sometimes they may have white markings on the head. It is also very rare for a foal to be born in a chestnut color. The ponies are very strong and can almost be classed as lightweight coldbloods. They are excellent workhorses and riding horses. Originally the only means of transportation in the mountains, Mérens have preserved their sure-footedness, frugality, and undemanding nature today.

These ponies strongly resemble horses depicted in fifteen-thousand-year-old cave drawings from Labastide, Lascaux, and Niaux in southwestern France, so it is presumed this breed is exceptionally old.

Mongolian

Height: 51–57 inches

Color: all colors, with dorsal stripe and dark mane

Origin: Mongolia

Mongolian horses are very closely related to Przewalski's horses.

The Mongolian horse is very similar to the Przewalski's horse. It is stocky with short but strong legs, a large head, and a very long mane and tail. The tail hair is strong enough to be braided into rope, and it can also be used for violin bows. The hooves are very sturdy, so very few animals wear horseshoes. Mongolian horses have relatively shallow and short movements and are good for riding.

People in Mongolia have always attached great importance to these horses: their milk was fermented and used for drinking, and the horses were also used as a source of meat and leather. They were an important livelihood for the Mongolian nomads for centuries. The Mongolian conqueror Genghis Khan used these horses in all his military campaigns. These small horses carried grown men and their war equipment halfway across the world.

These docile Mongolian horses have become very rare, but they adapt quickly to new environments and easily lose their fear of people.

103

Mustang

Height: 53–59 inches

Color: all colors

Origin: North America

Most mustangs live in pony reserves.

The Spanish conquistadors brought their horses to America. Before Columbus discovered America, there were no native horses. Many of the horses brought from Europe—from which mustangs originated—were feral. The name *mustang* comes from the Spanish *mestenos*, which means "adoptable stranger." In the United States, there are about forty thousand wild mustangs; however, for some years, their numbers have been controlled by driving them into traps by helicopter and then giving them to new homes for "adoption." But it is not as simple as it sounds: because they have grown up wild, mustangs can be very difficult to break in. They are relatively small and stocky, and their hair is mostly rather coarse, but some mustangs resemble the nobler Spanish horses or Berbers.

The red roan color, a reddish brown coat with coarse white hair, mainly occurs in mustangs and quarter horses.

New Forest Pony

Height: 49–58 inches
Color: all colors
Origin: England

The New Forest pony is a typical moor and mountain pony from England.

The New Forest ponies are from the New Forest in southern England. This former hunting area is now a popular tourist destination. There, New Forest ponies live semiwild alongside cattle and feed on sedges, heather, and reeds. The New Forest pony is one of the largest British mountain and moorland ponies and so are used as riding horses for adults. Generally speaking, the New Forest ponies are rather mixed, both in color and type; each pony is unique. Again and again, strange horses were released in the New Forest, and then they bred with the ponies. The larger stallions were allowed to stay with the herd while the New Forest stallions were shot, in order to increase the size of the breed. As varied as the New Forest ponies may be today, they all have a friendly nature and are suited as driving horses. Because they have always been crossed with other horse breeds, this pony is more closely related to the sport horses than any other mountain and moorland pony today. This has ensured they are more in demand and has preserved them against extinction.

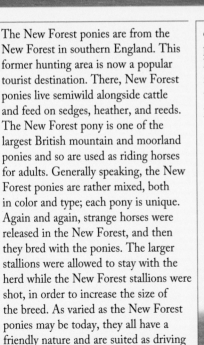

Polo Pony

Height: 61–62 inches

Color: all colors

Origin: Argentina

Polo is one of the oldest team sports in the world.

Polo ponies wait to begin the game.

In the nineteenth century, polo, a game native to Central Asia, became popular in Europe and America. In South America, horses suited to this sport were specially bred. The polo pony is a hybrid of the Argentine workhorse, the Criollo, and the English Thoroughbred. Originally, polo ponies were smaller; they were classed as "real" ponies, while the average height today is about sixty-one inches. Polo ponies have an enormously powerful sprint and are very quick at turning and stopping. They are bred according to their polo-playing abilities. There is no actual polo pony breed as such, but horses suitable for polo are crossed. Polo is one of the oldest team sports in the world and has been around for more than twenty-six hundred years, yet it has not changed very much. Initially, polo was a kind of fighting game, and therefore a very tough game. This type of polo is still practiced today. Horses undergo exceptionally high levels of stress during polo games, so it is somewhat doubtful whether the sport actually takes into account the welfare of the animal.

106

Pottok Pony

Height: 47–58 inches

Color: pinto, brown, and chestnut

Origin: Basque Country (France and Spain)

There are no white horses in the Pottok breed.

The Pottok pony comes from the Basque Country. Little is known about its ancestry, but there are prehistoric cave paintings of these ponies in French and Spanish Basque Country. Today Pottoks live semiwild in the mountains of the Basque provinces. The rugged mountains mean they have to be sure footed and sturdy—only the hardiest among them survive. For centuries, these ponies helped smuggle goods across the Pyrenees and also proved their resilience working in coal mines.

In the 1970s, Pottoks became a protected, registered breed of the French Association Nationale du Pottok (ANP). In France, the medium-sized type does very well in jumping and dressage events and also pony driving competitions. Particularly popular are the pintos; they have been named a separate type. Pottoks are grouped into standard Pottoks, pinto Pottoks, and double Pottoks. Double Pottoks are somewhat larger.

Przewalski's Horse

Height: 51–57 inches
Color: dun
Origin: Asia

Przewalski's horses live in Mongolia.

Przewalski's horses, also called Mongolian wild horses, are a very primitive breed. They are named after the Russian explorer Colonel Nikolai Przewalski, who discovered them during a trip to Mongolia in 1878.

The Przewalski's horse is gray dun or yellow dun with a lighter-colored muzzle. It has a dark dorsal stripe on the back and darker, striped legs. These horses are not very large, but they are extremely strong. They have short necks and shaggy manes. They are descendants of wild horses. Their original habitat was the high plains of Central Asia. Unfortunately, the original wild horses of this breed are now extinct in the wild and only exist in various animal parks and zoos. Since 1990, efforts have been made to reintroduce them into the wild with some success.

A typical feature of the Przewalski's horse is the lighter-colored muzzle.

Shetland Pony

Height: 34–42 inches
Color: all colors
Origin: Shetland Islands

Shetland ponies have great longevity. A thirty-year-old Shetland pony is not unheard of.

Shetland ponies come from the Shetland Islands, which lie to the north of Scotland. They are the oldest breed of horse in Britain. They are not artificially bred to be small but became naturally stunted due to the extremely harsh climate of the islands. In the nineteenth century, they were used to work in mines.

If they get bored, Shetland ponies can become very overweight and sometimes also impudent; they need to be given meaningful tasks. Many of them can jump outstandingly well.

Miniature Shetlands, a breed in their own right, are smaller still; they barely reach thirty-four inches in height. Mini Shetland ponies are hardly toy horses though; they can pull one and a half times their own body weight and are therefore excellent driving horses.

A Shetland pony's intelligence should not be underestimated.

Sorraia

Height: 55–59 inches

Color: yellow dun or mouse gray with a dorsal stripe and zebra markings on the legs

Origin: Portugal

It was long believed that Sorraias were the ancestors of Iberian horses.

The Sorraia is an Iberian wild horse. However, this breed is not, as was formerly believed, the ancestor of the Iberian horse. The Sorraias are an independent breed of wild horses that are thought to have originated from Tarpan ponies.

Sorraias were ridden by Portuguese shepherds for many centuries and therefore are capable of traveling for extended distances without too much trouble. Extreme weather changes and food shortages are well tolerated by the Sorraias; they are very resilient. Their origin is the tributary of the Tagus River joining the Sorraia River.

Unfortunately, these agile and versatile small horses have become very rare today, and they are now threatened with extinction. The convex head profile and long faces of the Sorraias may not necessarily correspond to modern equine beauty ideals, but their canter is really quite something to see. Many Sorraias even have a predisposition for the tölt.

Tarpan

Height: 51 inches
Color: dun
Origin: Eastern Europe

Tarpan is a Russian word meaning "wild horse."

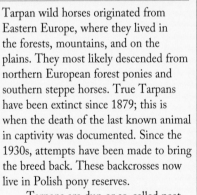

Tarpan wild horses originated from Eastern Europe, where they lived in the forests, mountains, and on the plains. They most likely descended from northern European forest ponies and southern steppe horses. True Tarpans have been extinct since 1879; this is when the death of the last known animal in captivity was documented. Since the 1930s, attempts have been made to bring the breed back. These backcrosses now live in Polish pony reserves.

Tarpans are dun or so-called peat brown. They have long dark manes and darker-colored legs. The Tarpan's outward appearance is very primitive: it has a medium-sized head; a short, thick neck; and a relatively straight back, similar to a Fjord horse. The legs are quite thin but very healthy and hardy. Tarpans are sure footed and persevering. Their descendants include the Polish Koniks, and it is possible to see the similarities. Tarpans can only survive in nature reserves because they were hunted relentlessly.

111

Welsh Pony

Height: up to 54 inches

Color: all colors except pinto; often white

Origin: Wales

Welsh ponies are divided into four different groups: A, B, C, and D.

Welsh ponies have lived in the British Isles since ancient times, most likely since the Celtic settlement in Wales. They come in four different types. Section A is the Welsh mountain pony in its ancestral form, from which all other types have emerged. The Section B Welsh pony originated from a crossing between Welsh mountain mares and the Berber stallion named Sahara. It is a riding pony or show type and is now mainly used as a riding and jumping pony for children or for driving carts. Much value is placed on the riding abilities of this breed. Nevertheless, due to its temperament, this pony is not suitable as a beginner horse.

The Section C Welsh pony of cob type is a miniature version of the Welsh cob—Section D—and originated from a cross between Powys cobs, the ancestors of today's Welsh cobs, and Welsh mountain ponies. This breed was used as a packhorse and driving horse in its homeland but is now mainly popular as a compact children's pony.

Welsh Mountain Pony

Height: up to 50 inches

Color: all colors except pinto; often white

Origin: Wales

One legendary pony of this breed was a Welsh mountain mare that lived to the age of forty-one and gave birth to thirty-five foals during her lifetime.

The Welsh mountain pony (Section A) is the foundation from which all other Welsh pony groups were bred. Originally the packhorse and riding horse of Celtic shepherds, it was also used in the second half of the nineteenth century in the coal mines. Today, it is a popular and versatile children's pony that has an above-average jumping ability.

Section A Welsh ponies are extremely attentive and receptive but also hot blooded and lively. Some ponies act like miniature Arabians because at certain times in history, this breed was crossed with Arabians. The ponies are often less than forty-eight inches tall but are permitted to be up to fifty inches in size. Larger Welsh mountain ponies can also be classed as Welsh ponies, but the reverse is not allowed: a Welsh pony that is too small cannot be classed as a Welsh mountain pony.

A Welsh mountain pony is a great beginner pony for children.

113

Welsh Cob

Height: 55–60 inches

Color: all colors except pinto

Origin: Wales

The Welsh cob is sometimes taller than the official pony measurement of fifty-eight inches.

The Welsh cob, the Section D Welsh pony, is a strong pony with a noble expression. The Welsh cob has an attractive, small head; a strong body; plenty of drive from the hindquarters; and an impressive trot with a high knee action. From this, it is possible to see the Welsh cob's relation to the Hackney; the were crossed with Hackneys in 1900. A crossing with Spanish horses is suspected The Welsh cob is suitable for agricultural work as well as coach driving, hunting, o for the military. Leisure riders and young beginner riders both appreciate the cob. On the basis of its size and stature, the Welsh cob pony is also ideal as a riding horse for adults, where it has proven itself in many disciplines. Welsh cobs are not limited to dressage and driving competition success; they also have a talent for Western riding.

A Welsh cob is strong enough to carry an adult.

A Welsh cob demonstrates the typical Hackney trot.

115

Gypsy Vanner

Height: 53–59 inches

Color: almost exclusively pinto

Origin: Ireland and Northern England

Gypsy Vanners are also known as tinkers. The pinto patterns on their coats are also known as piebald.

British and Irish Romany were also known as *tinkers* in Ireland, which is where the alternate name for the Gypsy Vanner, the tinker pony, has come from.

No two Gypsy Vanners are the same; their coloring is completely individual.

At the end of the nineteenth century, the caravan came into fashion, but it was too heavy to be pulled by donkeys. The Romany acquired pinto horses from various breeding associations, which were unwanted due to their piebald markings, and from these horses, they created their own breed.

The colorful coat pattern of each piebald horse is unique, so one horse can be easily distinguished from the others. The Romany saw the advantage of this special coloring and bred Gypsy Vanner purposefully to tow their wagons.

There is no official studbook for Gypsy Vanners, therefore each horse is quite different from another. Besides its colorful coat, another typical feature of the breed is its heavy feathering on the legs. The Gypsy Vanner usually has a large head, often with a convex nose profile, and is very strong. The croup is broad and often divided in the middle; this is called a split croup.

Donkey

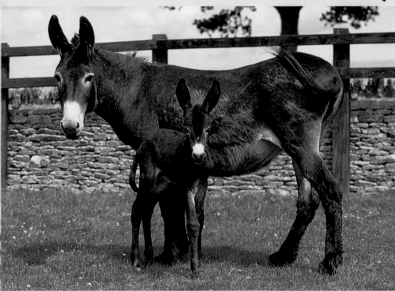

Height: 63 inches

Color: gray, brown, black, and spotted

Origin: France, Spain, Egypt

Almost all donkeys have a dark stripe that forms a cross down the back and across the shoulders, and many have zebra stripes on their legs.

These are miniature donkeys.

Donkeys are a distinctly different species from horses. Originating in North Africa, they have been bred and kept as domestic animals since the tenth century.

Donkeys have longer ears than horses, and the tail ends in a thick tassel. The color of their fur is usually gray, often with a trace of white on the back and belly. There are, however, also white, black, brown, and even spotted donkeys.

Donkeys are divided into different groups according to their size. Miniature donkeys are up to forty-one inches tall. Standard donkeys are up to fifty-three inches tall. Giant donkeys are more than fifty-three inches tall. Giant donkeys also come in different types that are specially bred and have their own breed registration. The Poitou donkey is fifty-three to sixty-one inches tall and is dark brown with golden spots. They have a white muzzle, white spots, and a white belly. With a weight of more than 880 pounds they are the heaviest donkeys in the world. The Catalan donkey is up to sixty-three inches tall and is black with small, brown markings, or bay with white silvery fur around the eyes, the mouth, and on the lower abdomen. The Andalusian donkey can also weigh up to 880 pounds and has various white markings. This breed most likely originated from the large white Egyptian donkeys. The Martina Franca donkey is black with white markings around the eyes, muzzle, and lower abdomen and is up to sixty-one inches tall. It is similar to the Catalan donkey.

The large white Egyptian donkey is only between forty-seven and fifty-five inches tall and is usually white to light gray. Arabian donkeys are similar in temperament to Arabian horses. The mammoth jacks are the only American donkey breed. They got their name from a male Catalan donkey, a jackass, called Mammoth.

117

Gaited Horses

< Icelandic horses live **wild herds in Iceland,** **well as in the mountai** **of California.**

> The Missouri fox **trotter was approved** **as the official state** **horse in 2002. To date,** **it is the main means o** **transportation for the** **Amish community.**

Gaited horses are breeds that have the natural ability to perform one of the smooth-to-ride, intermediate-speed, four-beat horse gaits collectively referred to as ambling gaits. All horse breeds are able to gallop and canter, but their ability to trot and pass is not always equal. Some breeds can only perform the diagonal gaited trot, others only the lateral, and some breeds are able to perform both types of gaits. The tölt is a four-stroke lateral gait. The steps taken between either the front feet or rear feet are leaping—there is a moment of time when neither front foot nor neither rear foot is on the ground.

In the saddle tölt, the steps taken between either the front feet or rear feet are momentarily supported by the other front or rear foot.

According to some scientific studies, two-thirds of all horses can be classed as gaited horses. There are about forty breeds of tölting horses. The Icelandic horse is probably the best known.

> To Whom Are Gaited Horses Suited?

Gaited horses are very well suited for people who want a comfortable gait or perhaps have a back problem—the gaited horse is usually very comfortable to ride. However, riders do need to be fairly experienced to ride a gaited horse because the various gaits are not always easy to handle.

Furthermore, not all horses that are gaited are bred simply to perform the saddle tölt. Some have very spectacular, high movements that may very well twist and turn the rider in the saddle. The most expressive equine movements

their individual gaits evaluated. Most gaited horses are not suited to classical dressage and jumping events because their trot is not correct according to the requirements of the dressage judges, and their jumping ability is usually average at best. Instead, gaited horses are suited to long-distance races and are ideal terrain and trail riding horses. When it comes to temperament, there are different breeds to suit different riders.

mostly belong to gaited horses, which makes them suitable for equestrian sport. They have their own competition scene, where they first undergo tests to have

‹ Icelandic horses have enormously thick forelocks (bangs) and manes, which give them protection during harsh winters in their homeland.

‹‹ Gaited horses can also gallop.

119

Aegidienberger

Height: 55–59 inches

Color: all colors

Origin: Aegidienberg stud farm, Germany

The idea to cross Icelandic horses with Peruvian Pasos was formed during Walter Feldmann's visit to Peru.

In the late 1970s, Walter Feldmann crossed Icelandic horses with Pasos at the stud farm in Aegidienberg, Germany, using the classic genetic method to breed a five-eighths cross. A pure Peruvian Paso stallion was mated with a pure Icelandic mare to produce the first generation (F1). The F1 generation was then crossbred with a pure Icelandic horse, resulting in the R1 generation. Finally, the F1 and R1 generations were crossed to produce the modern Aegidienberger, which has five-eighths Icelandic blood and three-eighths Peruvian Paso blood. The Aegidienberger is larger than the Icelandic horse but still small and robust enough to travel through rough terrain.

The Aegidienberger is medium sized, tough, and long living, with an innately extensive gait. Aegidienbergers have a high leg action and can sometimes also perform the pace, a lateral two-beat gait. This breed is sure footed and fast. Aegidienbergers are usually dark in color with few markings and long manes but no leg feathering.

Because the breed is still very new, the Aegidienberger is presently a relatively rare sight in the stables.

American Saddlebred

Height: 59–63 inches
Color: brown, chestnut
Origin: Kentucky

American saddlebreds were known as Kentucky saddlers.

This breed originated in the eighteenth century in Kentucky, through the refining of imported horses from American settlers. The result was an elegant yet hardy workhorse. Initially, the tireless American saddlebred was bred to work on horse ranches. Later it was used by the U.S. cavalry in the Civil War.

Today, saddlebreds are specially bred as show horses, where they demonstrate their natural disposition to tölt and pass. The breed is allowed to grow longer hooves than in other disciplines and is shod with pads and special shoes. Beautiful though it may appear, the American saddlebred has an unnaturally upright tail; this is created by a small but controversial tail setting operation.

The high action of the front leg is typical of American saddlebreds.

121

Icelandic Horse

Height: 51–57 inches

Color: all colors, including pinto

Origin: Iceland

Icelandic horses can even tölt on ice.

Icelandic horses originate from Iceland. Approximately forty-five thousand Icelandic horses live on the island today. These horses descended from horses that the Vikings brought to the island. Icelandic horses are capable of four gaits: walk, trot, canter/gallop, and tölt. (The canter and gallop are considered one gait by Icelandic horse registries.) There are a few five-gaited horses that can also perform the pace. The tölt is a four-stroke step, which is fast yet comfortable and flowing for the rider. Because there is always at least one foot on the ground,

the momentum of the saddle is very smooth. With the pace, the outer pairs of legs are set down simultaneously. The flying pace is very fast—often as fast as the gallop, reaching speeds of up to thirty miles per hour.

Icelandic horses are not just found in Iceland but are now frequently bred in other countries, such as Germany. These small, hardy ponies have been incredibly popular with leisure riders for many years now. Icelandic horses come in all colors. Pinto, palomino, and dun are common. Larger Icelandic horses are more than capable of carrying an adult. The smaller and lighter Icelandic horses are bred for equestrian sporting events and have too much of a lively temperament for recreational riders.

Icelandic horses are very hardy and are rarely kept in stables.

Mangalarga Marchador

Height: 58–61.5 inches

Color: all colors

Origin: Brazil

Mangalarga Marchadores are natural tölters.

Mangalarga Marchadores, simply called Marchadores, are naturally able to perform the *marcha* gait, a four-stroke gait. They do not usually trot, but they can perform the *marcha batida* and the *marcha picada*, in the form of a step and gallop gait. The marcha batida is a tölting trot and the marcha picada is purely a four-stroke gait.

The Mangalarga Marchadores originated from Brazil, where native mares (that were a result of a cross between Berbers and Portuguese horses) were crossed with an Altér Real stallion in the eighteenth century. The Iberian origin can be clearly seen today in the Mangalarga Marchador horses.

The head has a slightly convex nose profile, like that of an Iberian horse. In their homeland, they were specially bred for farmwork and riding, so a gentle gait was of particular importance. Brazilian farmworkers had to travel long distances without their horses tiring. Perseverance and beauty were also required characteristics. Mangalarga Marchador horses have an easygoing temperament, an uncomplicated nature, and are suitable for almost all leisure disciplines.

Mangalarga Marchadores come in all colors, including pinto. The breed's small size and friendly character makes it a popular leisure horse.

Missouri Fox Trotter

Height: 58–62 inches

Color: all colors; often chestnut or brown with markings

Origin: Missouri

Missouri fox trotters are mainly bred in Missouri and Arkansas.

The Missouri fox trotter is a Western horse with a colorful history. Morgan horses, Arabians, Tennessee walkers, and American saddlebreds were used to create this breed. The most notable feature of the Missouri fox trotter is his responsiveness. The flat-foot walk is a natural gait, typical to the breed and especially fast, yet comfortable for the rider. While performing the fox trot, the horse runs so that his front legs are stepping and his back legs are trotting; this is known as a broken gait. Using this unique style, the Missouri fox trotter can reach seven and a half miles per hour. For some people, the Missouri fox trotter is their main means of transportation: the Amish do not use cars but instead use horses and carriages.

125

Paso Fino

Height: 55–60 inches

Color: all colors

Origin: Dominican Republic, Puerto Rico, and Colombia.

The Paso Fino descends from horses brought to America by Spanish conquistadores and strongly resembles its Iberian ancestors.

Brio is a term that describes this horse's pleasant character.

The Paso Fino is used in his homeland as a workhorse and show horse and is separated into three different types: pleasure, performance, and classic. The pleasure type is a leisure horse for pleasant, smooth riding along railways and roads. The performance type is more fiery, so it is easier to motivate. The classic type is the most motivated of all, with very quick, short bursts of movement. The gaits for the first two types of Paso Fino are the *paso corto* (working pace) and *paso largo* (quick, four-stroke variant). The Paso Finos not only tölt, but they also have a gentle trot and an exemplary gallop. For Paso Finos, as well as Peruvian Pasos, much value is placed on the *brio*, a pleasant nature and temperament. In contrast to the Peruvian Pasos, Paso Finos do not display *termino*, a kind of sideways, outward movement of the forelegs. Paso Finos are traditionally ridden with a type of bitless headgear called a hackamore. While a bridle has a bit riders use to control the horse, a hackamore has a noseband called a bosal.

Peruvian Paso

Height: 55–60 inches
Color: all colors
Origin: Peru

Peruvian Pasos and Paso Finos are of the same origin.

The Peruvian Paso descends from Iberian horses. The special feature of the breed is its ability to tölt, which is 100 percent genetic. The types of tölt are differentiated as the *paso llano*, a slow, clear gait with four equal beats, and the *sobrandando*, which is a faster gait involving a pause between the front foot of one side to the back foot of the other side.

In Peru, the Peruvian Pasos were the only means of transportation for many years. The horses had to be hardy and sure footed but also easy to ride without too much effort.

A key feature of the breed is their so-called *brio*, a mixture of pride, attentiveness, self-confidence, and the desire to please people. This mixture is what makes the horses so easy to ride. Another feature of the Peruvian Paso is the *termino*, a gait where the forelegs roll to the outside when the horse steps forward. This affords the rider an almost vibration-free, smooth ride.

A Peruvian Paso performs the *sobrandando*.

127

Spotted Saddle Horse

Height: 60–65 inches
Color: pinto
Origin: United States

Spotted **is another term for pinto.**

All spotted saddle horses have the same thing in common—an attractive pinto pattern.

Spotted saddle horses are selected for breeding according to their gait ability and pinto pattern. They are not actually a specific breed but are bred regardless of their breed or descent. This means that each horse is very unique, but the one thing they all have in common is their gait ability and pinto pattern. The breed is based on gaited horses from all other breeds but are thought to have originated from pinto Icelandic horses.

Spotted saddle horses crossed with Tennessee walkers are popular, but trotters and mustangs also play significant roles. The horses are systematically selected according to their color, gait, and performance. The National Spotted Saddle Horse Association supervises breeding worldwide and also keeps a herd of these horses. Spotted saddle horses are very popular as pleasure horses. They move at very comfortable gaits for riders. The most important gait of the spotted saddle horse is the "saddle gait," a soft four-beat gait. Spotted saddle horses are common in the United States and Canada and are gradually gaining popularity in Europe.

128

Tennessee Walker

Height: about 61 inches

Color: mostly black, brown, or white

Origin: Tennessee

The hooves of Tennessee walkers are permitted to grow long to support the gait.

A pinto Tennessee walker is a rare sight.

The Tennessee walker was bred by plantation owners as a workhorse. They needed comfortable horses that could walk long distances in the heat and that were also agile enough to move between the rows of plants in the fields. The plantation ambler finally emerged, which was crossed with Morgans, Thoroughbreds, saddlebreds, and trotters.

The Tennessee walker is a medium-sized horse with a high-set neck and a high-set tail and an innate ability as a gaited horse. The desired gaits for this breed are the flat walk (reinforced, sliding step), the running walk (same movement as the flat walk, but at a higher speed), and the canter (an energetic rocking chair canter). Tennessee walkers nod their heads at each step. The flat walk of Tennessee walkers is so fast that the nod is very pronounced.

129

Western Horses

< The original discipline of Western riding was cattle work.

> Western horses come in many colors.

>> A typical quarter horse has plenty of acceleration.

Among the first Western horses that originated in North America are quarter horses, Appaloosas, and paint horses. They are highly maneuverable and can accelerate very fast. These are qualities that the cowboys appreciated when cattle herding. Quarter horses are the most common breed of horse in the world.

> To Whom Are Western Horses Suited?

A Western horse is intelligent, sensitive, very willing to learn, very pleasant, and sociable. Such a horse is suited to almost every rider. With its gentle gaits, a Western horse is ideal even for a beginner.

The specialties of Western horses are rapid acceleration, twists, and spectacular stops, which all suit exercises in Western disciplines. This is what the Western horse breeds do best. For the classic equestrian sport, however, a Western horse is not really ideal: the flat movements do not correspond to the requirements of a dressage horse, which requires expansive, soaring kicks, and the Western horse's jumping ability is usually not as good as a warmblood.

For those who dream of participating in an endurance race with their horses, a quarter horse or an Appaloosa is not the appropriate

of direction. Thanks to this natural talent, many Western horses are very good at Western disciplines such as "cutting" or "working cow horse," where the horses work to herd cattle.

⌄ **A horse with "cow sense" works the herd.**

horse because the massive muscles of the Western breeds in the croup and hindquarters are a load that is not designed for endurance. Instead, Western horses have "cow sense." Much like herding dogs, these horses can preempt the movements of a cow and will drive it ahead or separate it away from the herd more or less independently. The rider of a horse with cow sense can, in this case, rely almost entirely on the horse and must become accustomed to the naturally abrupt and extreme changes

Appaloosa

Height: 57–63 inches
Color: spotted
Origin: United States

Some Appaloosas can perform the "walkaloosa" gait.

The Appaloosa is a typical Western horse: it is sure footed, hardy, fast, and has cow sense. Appaloosas are very popular with Western riders all over the world. Appaloosas have striped hooves, marbled skin, and a distinctive coat pattern. This pattern differs from horse to horse; for example, it could be anything from black leopard spots on a white horse to a spotted area on the croup of a brown or black horse.

Appaloosas were bred by the Nez Perce Indians of the Pacific Northwest. The name *Appaloosa* is derived from the Palouse River on whose banks the Nez Perce Indians once had their pastures. The Nez Perce are considered the only Indian tribe who specifically bred their own breed of horses.

Criollo

Height: 54–59 inches
Color: all colors
Origin: South America

Criollo is a collective term for South American workhorses and riding horses.

The Criollos are very similar in every South American country. The Chilean Criollo horses are stocky and tough. They are usually dun, brown, and chestnut. The Argentinian Criollo is found in all colors. In South America, there are more than one hundred known colors. Criollos are medium sized and compact. In their homelands, they work on ranches, and their manes and tails are often cropped so they do not get thorns and scrub stuck in them. The influence of Iberian moor horses, which were imported to Argentina, can be clearly seen, but they also have Percheron blood flowing through their veins. Among the Peruvian Criollos, there are three different types: the wiry, slight Costeno; the strong Morochuco; and the frugal Chola. In Brazil, a modern type called the Crioulo is bred, as well as Mangalargas and Campo Linos. The Llanero from Venezuela is similar to the Sorraia.

Criollos are suitable for Western riding as well as recreational riding or trekking. Criollos are also used as polo ponies. These friendly horses are particularly popular with leisure riders.

133

Curly Horse

Height: 55–61 inches

Color: all colors

Origin: North America

Curly horses are ideal for people who are allergic to animal fur.

The curly horse is also called the Bashkir curly, although they are probably not related to the Russian Bashkir, which sometimes also has curly hair. Curlies go back to a herd of curly mustangs discovered by a rancher from Texas on his land in 1898. The breed was officially recognized in 1971. Curly-haired horses have always appeared in the Sioux and the Crow breeds, but whether they are relatives of the curly horse is not clear.

Curly horses are ideal for people who are allergic to horses with normal, straight hair: the curly horse very rarely causes an allergic reaction. Because these horses are selected for breeding specifically according to their curls, curly horses come in different colors and different sizes, but they are usually between fifty-five and sixty-one inches tall. Curlies are quite strong and have wedge-shaped heads and muscular necks. They have rather thin manes, which they sometimes shed in the summer. Then once winter comes, the mane grows back. Curly horses are quite rare because two curly horses often produce foals that do not have curly hair.

Morgan Horse

Height: 57–60 inches

Color: mainly brown and chestnut

Origin: United States

The Morgan horse is considered to be the United States' oldest horse breed.

Morgan horses originated at the end of the eighteenth century from a single stallion that belonged to a farmer named Thomas Justin Morgan. This stallion, standing at only fifty-five inches tall, was sired by a Godolphin Barb and was thought to have been crossed with a Welsh cob. Morgan's stallion was exceptionally successful in tournaments and unusually hardy as a workhorse, so Morgan was asked to stud out his horse. The offspring inherited this horse's dominant genes, so the stallion soon sired many horses that strongly resembled the original Morgan horse. Three of the stallion's sons were also very successful. An entire new breed was created from a single horse! Morgan horses have also influenced other horse breeds such as trotters, saddle horses, and Tennessee walkers. Today, they are especially popular as show horses. They have high-set necks and lush, long manes as well as friendly and intelligent natures.

Quarter Horse

Height: 58–61 inches

Color: all colors except pinto

Origin: United States

The first quarter horses were bred in Virginia and the Carolinas.

Typical features of the quarter horse are the short, broad head; the powerful torso; the slightly sloping croup; and the well-muscled hindquarters.

The quarter horse is known as the quintessential Western horse and stands between fifty-eight and sixty-one inches tall, with a short, broad head and very well-muscled hindquarters. Quarter horses are mostly brown or chestnut, but they can also be dun, black, or fawn. Pinto versions have their own special breed name—paint horses.

The American quarter horse was originally used in a horse race that was a quarter mile long; this was a fast gallop over a short distance, with rapid acceleration.

Many quarter horses have cow sense, an instinct for cattle herding. The more pronounced the innate cow sense is in a horse, the more independently it is able to drive the cattle. Worldwide, there are more than 4 million registered quarter horses.

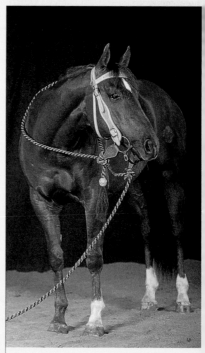

Quarter horses are one of the most popular horse breeds in the world.

Paint Horse

Height: 57–63 inches
Color: pinto
Origin: United States

Paint horses and quarter horses are identical except for the color of their coats.

Paint horses are simply pinto quarter horses; their origin, ancestry, and characteristics are the same. There are two highly recognizable patterns: the tobiano and overo. A tobiano has white legs, white markings across the back, and usually a dark head with some white. An overo has mostly dark legs, white markings that spread outward from the stomach rather than across the back, and a lot of white on the face, sometimes with blue eyes. A mixture of these types of markings is called tovero.

Many paint horses have a quarter horse mother or a quarter horse father, and sometimes even both parents are monochrome quarter horses. When a foal has too many white markings or the white markings are too large, then it is no longer considered a quarter horse—it is a paint horse. Originally, all of these horses were quarter horses, and it was only when the breed association refused to register the colorful spotted foals that owners founded their own breeding association for paint horses. Just like quarter horses, paint horses are fast, agile, and have a cow sense.

Pinto

Height: varies

Color: large patches of white with any other color

Origin: North America

Pinto is a Spanish word that means "painted" or "spotted."

A pinto is basically any horse that has patches of white and another color, no matter which breed it belongs to. However, according to the Pinto Horse Association of America, it must have at least four square inches of cumulative white anywhere on the body except below the knee or hock, from the ear to the corner of the mouth, and from the corner of the mouth to the chin. The white hair must also have pink skin underneath it. The pinto is classified as a horse if it is more than fifty-six inches tall at the withers. A pinto pony measures thirty-eight to fifty-six inches. A miniature B pinto is thirty-four to thirty-eight inches tall. And a miniature pinto measures thirty-four inches or less. The size of the white patch is reduced to only three square inches for ponies and two square inches for miniature horses.

Pintos are either tobiano or overo. The tobiano markings can be described as large spots of color over a white coat. The overo is the opposite pattern—white markings over a colored coat.

There are five classifications of pinto: stock, hunter, pleasure, saddle, and utility. The stock type is the Western horse among the pintos—paint horses and crossings with paint horses or quarter horses. The hunter type includes the Belgium warmblood, Hanoverian, and Thoroughbred. The pinto Arabian, Andalusian, and Morgan horse fall under the pleasure type. The saddle type includes gaited horses such as saddlebreds, Tennessee walkers, and Missouri fox trotters. Gypsy Vanners belong to the utility group.

139

Further Reading

Books

McBane, Susan. *The Illustrated Encyclopedia of Horse Breeds.* Minneapolis, Minn.: Wellfleet Press, 2008.

Paparelli, Luca, and Susanna Cottica. *Horses: Breeds, Cultures, Traditions.* New York: White Star Publishers, 2012.

Ransford, Sandy. *The Kingfisher Illustrated Horse and Pony Encyclopedia.* New York: Kingfisher, 2010.

Wright, Liz. *Beautiful Horses.* Lewes, East Sussex, U.K.: Ivy Press, 2013.

Internet Addresses

HorseChannel.com
http://www.horsechannel.com/horse-breeds/

American Museum of Natural History: Horse
http://www.amnh.org/exhibitions/past-exhibitions/horse

Animal Planet: Hoofed Mammals: Horse
http://animal.discovery.com/mammals/horse-info.htm

A-Z List of Horse Breeds

Translated from the German edition by Claire Mullen.

Edited and produced by Enslow Publishers, Inc.

Originally published in German.

© 2010 Franckh-Kosmos Verlags-GmbH & Co. KG, Stuttgart, Germany

Silke Behling, *Pferderassen: Die 100 bekanntesten Rassen*

Library of Congress Cataloging-in-Publication Data

Behling, Silke.
 [Pferderassen. English]
 Get to know horse breeds : the 100 best-known breeds / Silke Behling.
   p. cm. — (Get to know cat, dog, and horse breeds)
 Summary: "Discusses more than one hundred horse breeds categorized into groups according to temperament, build, and size: warm bloods, Throroughbreds, Baroque horses, cold bloods, small horses and ponies, gaited horses, and Western horses"— Provided by publisher.
 Audience: 011-
 Audience: Grades 7 to 8.
 Includes bibliographical references and index.
 ISBN 978-0-7660-4259-9
 1. Horse breeds—Juvenile literature. I. Title.
 SF291.B3413 2014
 636.1—dc23
 6680   2013007012

Paperback ISBN 978-1-4644-0461-0

Printed in the United States of America

112013 Bang Printing, Brainerd, Minn.

10 9 8 7 6 5 4 3 2 1

To Our Readers: We have done our best to make sure all Internet addresses in this book were active and appropriate when we went to press. However, the author and publisher have no control over and assume no liability for the material available on those Internet sites or on other Web sites they may link to. Any comments or suggestions can be sent by e-mail to comments@enslow.com or to the address on the back cover.

Every effort has been made to locate all copyright holders of material used in this book. If any errors or omissions have occurred, corrections will be made in future editions of this book.

All information in this book is given to the best of the author's knowledge. However, care during implementation is still required. The publishers, authors, and translators assume no liability for personal injury, property damage, or financial loss as a result of the application of the methods and ideas presented in this book.

♲ Enslow Publishers, Inc., is committed to printing our books on recycled paper. The paper in every book contains 10% to 30% post-consumer waste (PCW). The cover board on the outside of each book contains 100% PCW. Our goal is to do our part to help young people and the environment too!

Photo Credits: All color photos by Bob Langrish except Jean Christen/Kosmos, pp. 2 (middle), 44 (first photo in image bar), 46 (bottom); Ramona Dünisch, pp. 2 (top), 6 (first, second, and last photos in image bar), 10 (bottom), 11 (bottom), 12, 20 (bottom), 24 (bottom), 26, 29, 40, 41 (bottom), 42 (bottom), 46 (top), 54 (fourth and fifth photo in image bar), 55 (top), 60, 64 (fourth and fifth photos in image bar), 68, 73, 76, 77, 78, 80 (third photo in image bar), 82, 88 (bottom), 89 (bottom), 90 (top), 91, 98, 99, 100, 101, 103, 111, 120; Ramona Dünisch/Kosmos, pp. 44 (third photo in image bar), 45; Felix v. Döring/Kosmos, p. 89 (top); Alexander Frank, pp. 51, 116 (top); Klaus-Jürgen Guni/Kosmos, pp. 4 (top), 118 (first photo in image bar), 119 (bottom right), 122 (bottom), 130 (main photo and third, fourth, fifth, and last photos in image bar), 131 (top right and bottom), 136 (bottom), 137 (top); Sabine Keck, pp. 54 (third photo in image bar), 58 (bottom), 59 (bottom), 80 (second and last photos in image bar), 95, 114, 115; Bettina Klingmüller, p. 90 (bottom); Lothar Lenz/Kosmos, p 80 (fourth photo in image bar); Christof Salata/Kosmos, pp. 4 (bottom), 5 (bottom), 7 (top left, bottom); Shutterstock.com, p. 140; Horst Streitferdt/Kosmos, pp. 7 (top right), 45 (top), 81 (top right, bottom).

Cover Photo: Shutterstock.com (*main photo:* Shetland pony; *from top to bottom:* Friesian, quarter horse, Arabian, paint horse).